CASEBOOK S[...]

Eugene O'Neill

Three Plays

Mourning Becomes Electra
The Iceman Cometh
Long Day's Journey Into Night

A CASEBOOK

EDITED BY

NORMAND BERLIN

MACMILLAN

First published 1989

Published by
MACMILLAN EDUCATION LTD
Houndmills, Basingstoke, Hampshire RG21 2XS
and London
Companies and representatives
throughout the world

Typeset by Wessex Typesetters
(Division of The Eastern Press Ltd)
Frome, Somerset

Printed in Hong Kong

ISBN 0–333–42759–9
ISBN 0–333–42760–2 (pbk)

CONTENTS

System of Titling: here and in the Selection, exterior quotemarks are used for editorially devised captions. In other cases, the caption employs the original title of the writer's book, chapter or section of a book, article or essay (in some instances abbreviated from that), and it is displayed without exterior quotemarks.

TO THE MEMORY
OF
SAM SCHOENBERG

GENERAL EDITOR'S PREFACE

The Casebook series, launched in 1968, has become a well-regarded library of critical studies. The central concern of the series remains the 'single-author' volume, but suggestions from the academic community have led to an extension of the original plan, to include occasional volumes on such general themes as literary 'schools' and genres.

Each volume in the central category deals either with one well-known and influential work by an individual author, or with closely related works by one writer. The main section consists of critical readings, mostly modern, collected from books and journals. A selection of reviews and comments by the author's contemporaries is also included, and sometimes comment from the author himself. The Editor's Introduction charts the reputation of the work or works from the first appearance to the present time.

Volumes in the 'general themes' category are variable in structure but follow the basic purpose of the series in presenting an integrated selection of readings, with an Introduction which explores the theme and discusses the literary and critical issues involved.

A single volume can represent no more than a small selection of critical opinions. Some critics are excluded for reasons of space, and it is hoped that readers will pursue the suggestions for further reading in the Select Bibliography. Other contributions are severed from their original context, to which some readers may wish to turn. Indeed, if they take a hint from the critics represented here, they certainly will.

A. E. DYSON

INTRODUCTION

For most contemporary observers *Mourning Becomes Electra* (1931) marked the climax of what could be considered the first career of Eugene O'Neill (1888–1953). It was critically and commercially successful, and it gave the dramatist a big push towards his Nobel Prize of 1936. The play received the most enthusiastic reviews that O'Neill would read in his lifetime, and it further solidified his already secure reputation as America's most important dramatist. Behind him were the bold experiments of the 1920s, including the expressionism of *The Emperor Jones* (1920) and *The Hairy Ape* (1922), the masks of *The Great God Brown* (1925), the interior monologues of *Strange Interlude* (1928), but also the less experimental, less stylised, realistic plays, like *Beyond the Horizon* (1920), *Anna Christie* (1921) and *Desire Under the Elms* (1924). Before these came the one-act realistic 'sea' plays of the newcomer whose *Bound East for Cardiff* (1916), performed on the rickety boards of a wharf theatre in Provincetown, Massachusetts, made the Provincetown Players realise 'what we were for', and marked the beginning of modern American drama.

With *Mourning Becomes Electra* O'Neill was consciously competing with the ancient Greek dramatists, the dramatists he respected most because theirs was 'the one true theatre', and this competition caused him to labour over this play longer than any other – three years. The length of time is attributable in part to personal problems, but surely a more important reason was his clear recognition that in this massive play, a trilogy, he was giving modern America a play of great size and importance: the kind of play Greek audiences of the distant past witnessed as a celebration of religion and art. O'Neill's 'Work Diary'[*] records his intense engagement with his material. The result of his enormous labour – labour that at times made him wonder why he ever attempted 'the damn thing' – was a resoundingly positive response from most reviewers of the 1931 production. For them and for his audiences – who entered the Guild Theater, New York City, at 5 p.m. to see *The Homecoming*, then left for dinner, to return at 7 p.m. to see *The Hunted* and *The Haunted* until midnight – O'Neill had accomplished what he set out to do, what he continuously reminded himself that he had to do: 'to get

[*] Here and elsewhere in the Introduction, an asterisk within square brackets indicates reference to material in the Casebook selection. Numbered references to material or writers cited relate to the Notes for the Introduction, below.

modern psychological approximation of Greek sense of fate' into a play which a modern audience would 'accept and be moved by'. The reviewers of *Mourning Becomes Electra* represented in this Casebook, perhaps the most important American theatre reviewers working at the time – Stark Young, John Mason Brown, Brooks Atkinson, Robert Benchley – appreciated the heroic task O'Neill set for himself and applauded his large accomplishment. Later critical reaction to the play produced some negative voices, especially those of St John Ervine[*], who wondered how O'Neill had the audacity to compete with Aeschylus, and Eric Bentley[*], for whom the play's very largeness reveals O'Neill's basic weakness as a dramatist.

Mourning Becomes Electra remains a controversial play, not only because of its direct use of Greek tragedy and the intrinsic problem, clearly recognised by O'Neill, of bringing Greek myth to a modern stage, but also because of his use of Freud, which for some critics makes the play more clinical than tragical. What is not controversial is the recognition of the enormous energy that he expended on the play, his artistic ambitiousness, and the power of some of the play's individual scenes, especially the haunting moment at the trilogy's end, when Lavinia Mannon closes the door behind her in order to face her cursed family's ghosts. At that moment, Lavinia is O'Neill, entering his own house, ready to face his personal past. In that house, confronting his dead, O'Neill will write his most enduring and most 'modern' plays, *The Iceman Cometh* and *Long Day's Journey Into Night*.

So great was O'Neill's expenditure of energy on *Mourning Becomes Electra*, so emotionally draining was his act of creation, that he wrote his only pure comedy, *Ah, Wilderness!*, immediately after *Mourning Becomes Electra*, and he did so with great ease, as if he had to relieve himself of the terror of that dark house. After this comedy – the play in which he presents the kind of family life he would like to have had, the play whose setting is the same summer home in New London, Connecticut, occupied by the autobiographical Tyrones in *Long Day's Journey* – he wrote his worst play, *Days Without End* (1934). Here his main character, John Loving, affirms a faith in God, producing a highly positive ending which is laboured and false, rubbing against O'Neill's own basic doubts about religion and about man's vulnerable state in the scheme of things.

Then came O'Neill's 'silence', twelve years (from 1934 to 1946) without a new O'Neill play on Broadway. It seemed to many at the time that the positive Catholic ending of *Days Without End* sounded the death-knell of the dramatist's career. But during those silent years he was writing the great plays of his second coming – *The*

Iceman Cometh (1939), *Hughie* (1940), *Long Day's Journey Into Night* (1940), and *A Moon for the Misbegotten* (1943) – and was occupied with his projected cycle of eleven plays dealing with two hundred years of American history, from the Revolutionary War to the Depression of the 1930s. The cycle's overall title, 'A Tale of Possessors Self-Dispossessed', reveals the thrust of O'Neill's criticism of America, whose soul was being destroyed, he believed, by possessiveness and greed. Only one of the planned eleven plays was completed, *A Touch of the Poet*. Except for the typed third-draft manuscript of *More Stately Mansions*, which managed to survive, the manuscripts of the others, in different states of completion, were burned by O'Neill and his third wife, Carlotta Monterey O'Neill, before his death in 1953.

The 1946 Theatre Guild production of *The Iceman Cometh* – which he wrote in six months, from June through November 1939 – broke O'Neill's silence, and this is the very play which triggered the revival of interest in him in 1956, three years after his death. It therefore occupies an important place in any discussion of O'Neill's career and reputation. The play reveals a more 'modern' O'Neill, whose realism touches deeper recesses than ever before, whose comic sense is more obvious than ever before, and whose confrontation with existential issues is more effective than ever before.

However, the critical reception of the 1946 *Iceman* was mixed, for a number of reasons. The great anticipation of an O'Neill play after so long an absence from Broadway perhaps occasioned an understandable disappointment when the play arrived. The Theatre Guild production had some built-in problems, especially the spotty performance of James Barton as Hickey, a pivotal role that could make or break the play. Perhaps the sheer length of the play (four acts, four hours) worked against a clearly favourable reception, as did its pessimistic mood at a time when America had just come to the end of a world war and was looking forward to good times ahead. But enough important reviewers found it fine enough and powerful enough to recommend it to their readers, as the positive reviews of the influential Brooks Atkinson[*] and George Jean Nathan[*] indicate. The play had a modest run of 136 performances, and was to be the last O'Neill play to be performed on Broadway during the dramatist's lifetime.

The reaction to the 1956 Circle-in-the-Square *Iceman*, directed by José Quintero, with Jason Robards Jnr as Hickey, was unequivocally enthusiastic. (Brooks Atkinson's 1956 review for the *New York Times*[*] is typical.) No other O'Neill play had a longer run than this production, before or since – 565 performances. Coming only three years after his death, the enthusiasm marked an unusually early rebirth of his reputation, which was sadly muted during the ten years between the two *Iceman* productions. The reason for the play's success this time around prompts many speculations. Perhaps it was the play's direction by newcomer José Quintero, who displayed an instinctive understanding of the play's 'musical' qualities, the arrangement of sound and the repetition of phrase. Perhaps it was the stunning performance of Jason Robards Jnr, whose Hickey made theatre history and immediately proclaimed Robards as *the* O'Neill actor. Perhaps it was the intimate setting of the Circle-in-the-Square, seating only 200: a former Greenwich Village nightclub perfectly suited to the play's bar-room atmosphere. Perhaps America in 1956 was now ready for a play that expressed post-war despair and post-war existentialism. (It is no mere coincidence, I believe, that Broadway audiences saw both O'Neill's *The Iceman Cometh* and Samuel Beckett's *Waiting for Godot* in the same year.) Favourable receptions of subsequent productions of the play in later years have ensured its place as one of O'Neill's most enduring achievements – a reception exemplified by the Tynan and Wilkins reviews[*]. Through the years *The Iceman Cometh* has become the most discussed and most richly controversial play in the O'Neill canon, with critics offering intelligent, often passionate, appraisals, both pro and con (as our selection in Part Two, section 3 seeks to show).

Quintero's 1956 success with *Iceman* led Carlotta Monterey O'Neill to allow the young director to present *Long Day's Journey Into Night* on Broadway that same year. She had already given Yale University Press permission to publish the book version of the play in February 1956, and in that same month the play was performed and enthusiastically received in Sweden, a country that always offered O'Neill the most encouragement. O'Neill, not wanting his family to be displayed on the boards, had expressed his wish that this highly personal play should not be performed at any time, nor published until twenty-five years after his death. Carlotta disregarded his request when deciding to give the play to the world in 1956, much to the chagrin of the dramatist's friends and the Random House publishers to whom his request had been made. Justifiable or not, Carlotta's decision to have Quintero direct *Long Day's Journey* six months after he had produced the highly acclaimed *Iceman* absolutely ensured continuing admiration for the reborn O'Neill. Quintero's production, which opened in the Helen Hayes Theatre, Broadway, on 7 November 1956, received praise from almost all reviewers. Each of the actors was given high marks – Fredric March as James Tyrone, Florence Eldridge as Mary Tyrone, Jason Robards Jnr as

Jamie, Bradford Dillman as Edmund. Subsequent productions of the play have attracted the finest actors to the various roles, most notably Laurence Olivier and Jason Robards Jnr as James Tyrone, and Geraldine Fitzgerald and Colleen Dewhurst as Mary Tyrone. O'Neill's most autobiographical play, 'written in tears and blood . . . with deep pity and understanding and foregiveness for all the four haunted Tyrones', as he states in his dedication to Carlotta, has been acknowledged generally as his greatest play, for many the highest achievement in American realistic theatre.

Mourning Becomes Electra, *The Iceman Cometh* and *Long Day's Journey Into Night*, like most of the plays in O'Neill's long career, have been the focus of much critical attention, resulting in a wide range of diverse opinions about his dramatic art. This is understandable – a testimony to his high ambition, to his many attempts to extend the boundaries of his medium, to the challenges he poses to his actors and his audiences. He has been both championed and derided by some of the most important critics of our time. Among those on the plus side: T. S. Eliot, Edmund Wilson, Lionel Trilling, Clifford Leech, George Jean Nathan[*], Joseph Wood Krutch[*], John Gassner. Among those on the minus side: Mary McCarthy, Eric Bentley[*], Bernard DeVoto, St John Ervine[*], Francis Fergusson. Most of these critics, whether pro or con, have asserted that O'Neill lacked the language to accomplish successfully the large tasks he set for himself, perhaps taking their cue from O'Neill himself, who said, for example, that *Mourning Becomes Electra* 'needed great language to lift it beyond itself. I haven't got that'; and who, when speaking through Edmund Tyrone, says that he 'hasn't even got the makings' of a poet, that he is only able to 'stammer'. What must be acknowledged, perhaps strongly acknowledged because of such criticism, is that O'Neill's stage prose works *in the theatre*. Despite stretches of inflated or awkward prose, his language is usually effective enough to stir the emotions of his audience. No one who says his words on the stage mentions O'Neill's deficiencies. Jason Robards Jnr places the emphasis where it belongs: O'Neill wrote plays 'to be performed. He didn't write literature'. In recent years O'Neill's stage speech has been applauded in books written by such astute scholars of his work as Travis Bogard, John Henry Raleigh, Jean Chothia, Timo Tiusanen, and Egil Tornqvist, all represented in this Casebook. Like all giants, O'Neill has blemishes that seem more gross precisely because he is a giant of the theatre. His deficiencies will continue to be acknowledged and discussed, as they should be, but his position as the leading dramatist in the whole history of American theatre seems secure.

☆

Mourning Becomes Electra, as the climax of O'Neill's 'first' career, and *The Iceman Cometh* and *Long Day's Journey Into Night*, as the high points of his 'second' career, provide a revealing focus for a Casebook. Not only do these three plays allow us to examine the critical reception of O'Neill at crucial moments in his development, but they also clearly exhibit his power and ambition, his artistic preoccupations, his abiding aims. Exceeding the usual length of Broadway plays, and in fact of almost all modern plays, they evoke more than the usual amount of powerful emotion. *Mourning Becomes Electra* is an epic treatment of a New England family after the Civil War, a Greek-style trilogy filled with high passion, incestuous thoughts, murder, suicide, revenge. *The Iceman Cometh* takes four hours to orchestrate the alcohol-drenched pipe-dreams of the lodgers in a 1912 New York City saloon, 'The End of the Line Cafe', into which a salesman called Hickey, the play's Iceman, comes to sell Death. *Long Day's Journey* gives us a very long day – long because painful and heavy and endless, as well as the four hours playing time – in the New London summer home of the Tyrone family, also in the year 1912: a day in which each member of the family makes an agonising journey into night, the night of the play, the night of dreams, 'death'. (The year 1912 was the most crucial year in O'Neill's life. Aged 23, the dissolute son of the famous Irish-born actor James O'Neill attempted suicide in Jimmy-the-Priest's saloon in New York City, divorced his first wife, lived during the summer with his dope-filled mother and penurious father in New London, Connecticut, learned that he had tuberculosis, and entered a sanatorium on Christmas Eve of that year. He left it six months later with the belief that he must be 'an artist or nothing', after having read Strindberg for the first time, the writer 'who gave me the vision of what modern drama could be'.) Each of these harrowing mammoth plays has Death as its subject, mourning always becoming to O'Neill who, like *Iceman*'s Larry Slade, was 'a convert to death', and like Edmund Tyrone, was always 'a little in love with death'.

In each of these plays a heavy determinism pushes the characters along their dark paths. In *Mourning Becomes Electra* the Mannon family's curse, combined with the psychological determinism of Freud and the historical determinism of a New England Puritanism, controls the lives of the characters, forcing them to live and try to love in a world where the sun is always setting, in dark rooms where flickering candlelight reveals the portraits of the dead. In *The Iceman Cometh* the past controls the todays and tomorrows of Harry Hope's roomers, frozen to their conditions, filled with alcohol and pipedream, members of 'the tomorrow movement', literally at 'the last harbor'.

So too in *Long Day's Journey* the past causes the hellish life the Tyrones live today, both separately and together. As Mary Tyrone tells her husband, 'The past is the present, isn't it? It's the future, too. We all try to lie out of that but life won't let us.'

In each play Life itself points to the ultimate mysterious determinism. The words of Christine Mannon in *Mourning Becomes Electra* ring true: 'Why can't all of us remain innocent and loving and trusting? But life won't leave us alone. It twists and wrings and tortures our lives with others' lives until – we poison each other to death!' But nowhere is the idea better expressed than in Mary Tyrone's sad recognition: 'None of us can help the things life has done to us. They're done before you realize it, and once they're done they make you do other things until at last everything comes between you and what you'd like to be, and you've lost your true self forever.' This force that pushes man along a path of suffering and loss and frustration cannot be explained, remains secret, an idea O'Neill dramatises in these three plays and throughout his career. He is touching a universal thought, a universal feeling. In these plays his emphasis on Death, on the burdens of the past, on determinism, his staring at Life itself, his insistence that life somehow betrays us, forces us to share in the experience of the Mannons and of the 'family' of drunkards at Harry Hope's saloon and of the Tyrones. Their experience is a significantly lived experience, complex and deep, mirroring the experience of all of us. O'Neill himself, early in his career, acknowledged his 'feeling for the impelling, inscrutable forces behind life which it is my ambition to at least faintly shadow at their work in my plays'.[1] In his three big plays he does more than faintly shadow these forces; in these plays shadow becomes substance.

In all three plays – for many critics the three most important plays in O'Neill's canon – he displays his instinctive knowledge of what works in the theatre. Stripped of the theatrical devices he used in his experimental plays – although still playing with 'mask-like' faces in *Mourning Becomes Electra* – these plays are products of a realistic imagination working with sound and light and guesture and movement and setting, to produce highly emotive situations, highly charged moments. In each play he makes enormous demands on his audience, forcing it to listen to the talk of members of a family for hours, stuck in a room or in a saloon or on the steps of a house, and makes the largest demands on his actors as well. As we listen, as we enter deeper into their lives, we begin to care about these people, to feel warmth and compassion. This is more true of our response to the Tyrones and the *Iceman* characters than to the

INTRODUCTION 17

Mannons, but by play's end we care about Lavinia too. O'Neill's dramatic art turns his compassion and understanding to our compassion and understanding.

These three plays offer a realistic presentation of life, not by 'holding the family kodak up to ill-nature', what O'Neill condemned as a characteristic of the old realism, nor by giving us 'the banality of surfaces',[2] but rather by aiming for 'a drama of souls'.[3] In one of the most important statements that he made after his work was over, he insisted that he was

always trying to interpret Life in terms of lives, never just lives in terms of character. I'm always acutely conscious of the Force behind – Fate, God, our biological past creating our present, whatever one calls it – Mystery certainly – and of the one eternal tragedy of Man in his glorious, self-destructive struggle to make the Force express him instead of being, as an animal is, an infinitesimal incident in its expression. And my profound conviction is that this is the only subject worth writing about and that it is possible – or can be – to develop a tragic expression in terms of transfigured modern values and symbols in the theatre which may to some degree bring home to members of a modern audience their ennobling identity with the tragic figures on the stage. Of course, this is very much of a dream, but where the theatre is concerned, one must have a dream, and the Greek dream in tragedy is the noblest ever![4]

It was 'the Greek dream in tragedy' that O'Neill had in mind when he wrote his blatantly 'Greek' trilogy, Mourning Becomes Electra. But that dream was also his when he was writing the two autobiographical plays, Iceman and Long Day's Journey. They observe even more strictly than Mourning Becomes Electra the classical unities, they incrementally uncover secrets of the past, they make an audience feel 'the Force behind'. Like all great tragedy, these three 'classical' plays celebrate mystery and the nobility of man's struggle and endurance.

And like all great drama, they appeal to our emotions. O'Neill believed that 'our emotions are a better guide than our thoughts. Our emotions are instinctive. They are the result not only of our individual experiences but of the experiences of the whole human race, back through the ages.'[5] O'Neill insisted that the 'truth usually goes deep. So it reaches you through your emotions'. He forever pursued the *truth* of man's existence by appealing to *emotions*. He said he would 'never be influenced by any consideration but one: Is it the truth as I know it – or, better still, feel it?'[6] He himself felt deeply what he wrote, and here the autobiographical pressures exerted on his work – especially in Long Day's Journey and Iceman, but also in Mourning Becomes Electra – must be acknowledged. These

personal pressures invest his characters with a dimension of feeling
that cannot be analysed. The intensity of his personal commitment
to what he is dramatising affects the emotions of his audience. The
sincerity of his attempt to express the frustrations of our lives, the
mystery of the force behind, at times the absurdity of our condition,
often seem palpable. Always aware that the darkly inexpressible
cannot be expressed, giving voice to his inadequacy through the
words of Edmund Tyrone – 'I couldn't touch what I tried to tell
you just now. I just stammered. That's the best I'll ever do, I mean
if I live. Well, it will be faithful realism, at least. Stammering is the
native eloquence of us fog people' – he nevertheless managed in his
best work, certainly in the three big plays treated in this Casebook,
to produce works of art that can stand with the best in modern
drama.

NOTES

1. Eugene O'Neill, in a letter to Barrett Clark, in Oscar Cargill, N. Bryllion Fagin,
and William J. Fisher (eds), *O'Neill and his Plays* (New York, 1961), p. 100.
2. O'Neill, in a playbill for Strindberg's *The Spook Sonata*, 3 January 1924, in
Cargill *et al.*, op. cit., p. 108.
3. O'Neill, phrase found in 'Memoranda on Masks', in ibid., p. 116.
4. O'Neill, in a letter to Arthur Hobson Quinn, in ibid., p. 125.
5. Mary B. Mullett, 'The Extraordinary Story of Eugene O'Neill', *American
Magazine*, xciv (November 1922), p. 34.
6. Barrett H. Clark, *Eugene O'Neill: The Man and His Plays* (New York, 1929),
p. 195.

PART ONE

Mourning Becomes Electra

1. COMMENT BY O'NEILL

I 'OH, FOR A LANGUAGE . . . !' (1929)

. . . Oh, for a language to write drama in! For a speech that is dramatic and isn't just conversation! I'm so straight-jacketed by writing in terms of talk! I'm so fed up with the dodge-question of dialect! But where to find that language? . . .

SOURCE: extract from letter to Joseph Wood Krutch (27 July 1929); quoted in Arthur & Barbara Gelb, *O'Neill* (New York, 1962), p. 698.

II WORK DIARY (1926–31)

1. Spring 1926
Modern psychological drama using one of the old legend plots of Greek tragedy for its basic theme – the Electra story? – the Medea? Is it possible to get modern psychological approximation of Greek sense of fate into such a play, which an intelligent audience of today, possessed of no belief in gods or supernatural retribution, could accept and be moved by? –

2. October 1928 (Arabian Sea, en route for China)
Greek tragedy plot idea – story of Electra and family psychologically most interesting – most comprehensive intense basic human interrelationships – can be easily widened in scope to include still others.

3. November 1928 (China Sea)
Greek plot idea – give modern Electra figure in play tragic ending worthy of character. In Greek story she peters out into undramatic married banality. Such a character contained too much tragic fate within her soul to permit this – why should Furies have let Electra escape unpunished? Why did the chain of fated crime and retribution ignore her mother's murderess? – a weakness in what remains to us of Greek tragedy that there is no play about Electra's life after the

murder of Clytemnestra. Surely it possesses as imaginative tragic possibilities as any of their plots!

4.   April 1929 (Cap d'Ail, France)
Greek tragedy plot idea. – No matter in what period of American history play is laid, must remain a modern psychological drama – nothing to do with period except to use it as a mask – What war? – Revolution too far off and too clogged in people's minds with romantic grammar-school-history associations. World War too near and recognizable in its obstructing (for my purpose) minor aspects and superficial character identifications (audience would not see fated wood because too busy recalling trees) – needs distance and perspective – period not too distant for audience to associate itself with, yet possessing costume, etc. – possessing sufficient mask of time and space, so that audiences will unconsciously grasp at once, it is primarily drama of hidden life forces – fate – behind lives of characters. Civil War is only possibility – fits into picture – Civil War as background for drama of murderous family love and hate –

5.   April 1929 (Cap d'Ail)
(Greek plot idea) – Lay in New England small seaport, shipbuilding town – family town's best – shipbuilders and owners – wealthy for period – Agamemnon character town's leading citizen, Mayor before war, now Brigadier General Grant's Army – opening act of play day of Lee's surrender – house Greek temple front type that was rage in 1st half 19th century – (this fits in well and absolutely justifiable, not forced Greek similarity) – This home of New England House of Atreus was built in 1830, say, by Atreus character, Agamemnon's father – grotesque perversion of everything Greek temple expressed of meaning of life – (New England background best possible dramatically for Greek plot of crime and retribution, chain of fate – Puritan conviction of man born to sin and punishment – Orestes' furies within him, his conscience – etc.)
    Departures from Greek story – Electra loves Aegisthus – always fated to be mother's rival in love, always defeated – first for father's love, then for brother's, finally for Aegisthus – reason for Clytemnestra's hatred for Agamemnon sexual frustration by his puritan sense of guilt turning love to lust (she had romantic love for him before marriage) – omit Iphigenia and Chrysothemis from children – only Orestes and Electra – no Cassandra – keep exact family relationship of Aegisthus (first cousin Agamemnon) – keep general outline of rivalry, hatred, love, lust, revenge in past between Agamemnon's father, Atreus, and Aegisthus' father, Thyestes (in

legend Thyestes seduces Aerope, wife of Atreus) – hatred of Atreus
for brother – revenge – banishment – (keep general spirit of this but
pay no attention to details of legend) Clytemnestra persuades
Aegisthus against his will to help her murder Agamemnon (my
Aegisthus character weaker, more human and less evil character,
has conscience of sort) – method of murder, poison (woman's
weapon) – Aegisthus bears strong facial resemblance to Agamemnon
and Orestes – his resemblance to Orestes attracts Clytemnestra –
his resemblance to her father attracts Electra – Electra adores father,
devoted to brother (who resembles father), hates mother – Orestes
adores mother, devoted to sister (whose face resembles mother's) so
hates his father – Agamemnon, frustrated in love for Clytemnestra,
adores daughter, Electra, who resembles her, hates and is jealous of
his son, Orestes – etc. – work out this symbol of family resemblances
and identification (as visible sign of the family fate) still further –
use masks(?)

6.   *May 1929 (Cap d'Ail)*
(Greek plot idea) – Names of characters – use characteristic names
with some similarity to Greek ones – for main characters, at least –
but don't strain after this and make it a stunt – no real importance,
only convenience in picking – right names always tough job.
   Agamemnon – (Asa), (Ezra)
     Mannon
   Clytemnestra – Christine(?)
   Orestes – Orin
   { Electrâ Eleanor(?) Ellen(?) Elsa(?)
   { Laodicea – Lavinia (this sounds more like it) Vinnie (Called
     in family)
   Aegisthus – Augustus(?) Alan Adam
   Pylades – Paul(?) Peter(?)
   Hermione – Hazel – Hesther

7.   *May 1929 (Cap d'Ail)*
(Greek plot idea) – Title – 'Mourning Becomes Electra' – that is, in
old sense of word – it befits – it becomes Electra to mourn – it is
her fate, – also, in usual sense (made ironical here), mourning
(black) is becoming to her – it is the only color that becomes her
destiny –

8.   *May 1929 (Cap d'Ail)*
'Mourning Becomes Electra' – No chance getting full value material
into one play or even two – must follow Greek practice and make it

trilogy – first play Agamemnon's home-coming and murder – second, Electra's revenge on mother and lover, using Orestes to help her – third play, retribution Orestes and Electra.

Give each play a separate title – 'Mourning Becomes Electra' title for trilogy as whole – first play, 'Home-coming' – second,   (?) – third, 'The Haunted'.

9.   May 1929 (Cap d'Ail)
'Mourning Becomes Electra' – Technique – for first draft use comparatively straight realism – this first draft only for purpose of plot material into definite form – then lay aside for period and later decide how to go to final version – what departures necessary – whether to use masks, soliloquies, asides, etc. –

10.   20 June 1929 (Le Plessis, St Antoine-du-Rocher)
'Mourning Becomes Electra' – Finished scenario first play, 'Home-coming'.

11.   11 July 1929 (Le Plessis)
'Mourning Becomes Electra' – Finished scenario second play, 'The Hunted' – what an advantage it was (from a plotter's standpoint, at least) for authors in other times who wrote about kings – could commit murder without having to dodge detection, arrest, trial scenes for their characters – I have to waste a lot of ingenuity to enable my plotters to get away with it without suspicion! – still, even history of comparatively recent crimes (where they happen among people supposedly respectable) shows that rural authorities easily hoodwinked – the poisoning of Mannon in 'Homecoming' would probably never be suspected (under the same circumstances) even in New England town of today, let alone in 1865.

12.   August 1929 (Le Plessis)
'Mourning Becomes Electra' – Finished scenario third play, 'The Haunted' – have given my Yankee Electra tragic end worthy of her – and Orestes, too.

13.   September 1929 (Le Plessis)
Started writing 1st draft – 'Mourning Becomes Electra'.

14.   October 1929 (Le Plessis)
After several false starts, all rotten, think I have hit right line for first draft now.

15.   *21 February 1930 (Le Plessis)*
Finished 1st draft 'M.B.E.' – lay aside now for at least a month.

16.   *27 March 1930 (Le Plessis)*
Read over first draft 'M.B.E.' – scrawny stuff but serves purpose as
first draft – parts damned thrilling but lots more lousy – not enough
meat – don't like Aegisthus' character – hackneyed and thin – must
find new one – not enough of sense of fate hovering over characters,
fate of family – living in the house built by Atreus' hatred (Abe
Mannon) – a psychological fate – reading this first draft I get feeling
that more of my idea was left out of play than there is in it! – In
next version I must correct this at all costs – run the risk of going to
other cluttered up extreme – use every means to gain added depth
and scope – can always cut what is unnecessary afterwards – will
write second draft using half masks and an 'Interlude' technique
(combination 'Lazarus' and 'Interlude') and see what can be gotten
out of that – think these will aid me to get just the right effect –
must get more distance and perspective – more sense of fate – more
sense of the unreal behind what we call reality which is the real
reality! – The unrealistic truth wearing the mask of lying reality,
that is the right feeling for this trilogy, if I can only catch it! Stick
to modern tempo of dialogue without attempt at pretence of Civil
Wartime lingo. That part of 1st draft is right. Obtain more fixed
formal structure for first play which succeeding plays will reiterate –
pattern of exterior and interior scenes, beginning and ending with
exterior in each play – with the one ship scene at the center of the
second play (this, center of whole work) emphasizing sea background
of family and symbolic motive of sea as means of escape and release –
use townsfolk at the beginning of each play, outside house, as fixed
chorus pattern – representing prying, commenting, curious town as
an ever-present background for the drama of the Mannon family.
Develop South Sea Island motive – its appeal for them all (in various
aspects) – release, peace, security, beauty, freedom of conscience,
sinlessness, etc. – longing for the primitive – and mother symbol –
yearning for pre-natal non-competitive freedom from fear – make
this Island theme recurrent motive – Characterization – Exclude as
far as possible and consistent with living people, the easy superficial
characterization of individual mannerisms – unless these mannerisms
are inevitable finger-prints of inner nature – essential revelations.
This applies to main people of trilogy. Townsfolk, on the other
hand, should be confined to exterior characterization – main
characters too interior – Peter and Hazel should be almost characterless, judged from either of these angles – they are the untroubled,

contented 'good', a sweet, constant unselfconscious, untempted virtue amid which evil passion works, unrecognized by them – (until end) – but emphasized by their contrast. Resemblance of characters by use of masks intensify Mannon family resemblance between Ezra and Orin and Adam (and family portraits), and between Christine and Lavinia – peculiar gold-brown hair exactly alike in Lavinia and her mother – same as hair of the dead woman, Adam's mother, whom Ezra's father and uncle had loved – who started the chain of recurrent love and hatred and revenge – emphasize this motivating fate out of past – hair of women another recurrent motive – strange, hidden psychic identity of Christine with the dead woman and of Lavinia (in spite of her father – Mannon imitative mannerisms) with her mother – and of Adam with the Mannons he hates, as well as of Orin with his father – The chanty 'Shenandoah' – use this more – as a sort of theme song – its simple sad rhythm of hopeless sea longing peculiarly significant – even the stupid words have striking meaning when considered in relation to tragic events in play – In my scrawny first draft bare melodrama of plot runs away with my intent – this must be corrected in second draft – the unavoidable entire melodramatic action must be felt as working out of psychic fate from past – thereby attain tragic significance – or else! – a hell of a problem, a modern tragic interpretation of classic fate without benefit of gods – for it must, before everything, remain modern psychological play – fate springing out of the family –

17. 31 March 1930 (Le Plessis)
Start writing 2nd draft

18. 11 July 1930 (Le Plessis)
Finish 2nd draft – feel drained out – have been working morning, afternoon and night every day, without a single let-up – never worked so intensively over such a long period as I have on this damn' trilogy – wish now I'd never attempted the damn' thing – bitten off more than can chew? – Too close to it to see anything but blur of words – discouraged reaction natural now – after all, do know I was deeply moved by each play as I wrote it – that test has always proved valid heretofore – lay it aside now – we are off to Paris tomorrow – nice little vacation in dentist's chair scheduled! Best anodyne for pernicious brooding over one's inadequacies, that! – Anything else seems like the best of all possible when your nerves are prancing to sweet and low down of dentist's drill! –

19.   18 July 1930 (Le Plessis)
Read the trilogy – much better than I feared – but needs a lot more
work before it will be anything like right – chief thing, thought
asides now seem entirely unnecessary – don't reveal anything about
the characters I can't bring out quite naturally in their talk or their
soliloquies when alone – simply get in the way of the play's drive,
make the line waver, cause action to halt and limp – must be deleted
in toto – Warning! – always hereafter regard with suspicion hangover
inclination to use 'Interlude' technique regardless – that was what
principally hurt 'Dynamo', being forced into thought-asides method
which was quite alien to essential psychological form of its
characters – did not ring true – only clogged up play arbitrarily
with obvious author's mannerisms – saw this when I re-read it after
return from East – too late! 'Interlude' aside technique is special
expression for special type of modern neurotic, disintegrated soul –
when dealing with simple direct folk or characters of strong will and
intense passions, it is superfluous show-shop 'business'.

20.   19 July 1930 (Le Plessis)
Read trilogy again – don't like the soliloquies in their present
disjointed thought-prose formula – and my use of half masks on the
main protagonists seems to obscure meaning of resemblance between
characters instead of dramatically intensifying this meaning – masks
introduce other connotations not wanted these plays – have strong
feeling there should be much more definite interrelationship between
characters' masks and soliloquies, that soliloquies should be arbitrarily set in a stylized form that will be the exact expression of
stylized mask symbol – Rewrite all soliloquies in plays along this
line – introduce new ones so that soliloquies will recur in a fixed
pattern throughout, fitting into structural pattern repeated in each
play – try for prose with simple forceful repeating accent and
rhythm which will express driving insistent compulsion of passions
engendered in family past, which constitute family fate (always
remembering fate from within the family is modern psychological
approximation of the Greek conception of fate from without, from
the supernatural).

21.   20 July 1930 (Le Plessis)
Start rewriting, cutting out all asides, stylizing soliloquies as per
new conception – think I have hit on right rhythm of prose –
monotonous, simple words driving insistence – tom-tom from 'Jones'
in thought repetition –

22.   16 September 1930 (Le Plessis)
Finished rewriting – lay aside for a while – one thing I am certain
of right now, omitting asides has helped plays enormously –

23.   20 September 1930 (Paris)
Read and carefully reread this last stylized-soliloquies version –
absolutely convinced they don't do! – feel as I felt about asides in
version before this, that they held up plays, break rhythm, clog flow
of dramatic development, reveal nothing of characters' motives,
secret desires or dreams, that can't be shown directly or clearly
suggested in their pantomime or talk – some of these soliloquies are
gratifying as pieces of writing in themselves (most of them are not!)
but even then they don't belong – have no inherent place in
structure – they must come out – and with them the half-masks of
the Mannons must go too – obtrude themselves too much into the
foreground – introduce an obvious duality-of-character symbolism
quite outside my intent in these plays – and if I leave out soliloquies,
there is no excuse for these half-masks anyway – save for some
future play.

24.   21 September 1930 (Paris)
Scheme for revision and final version – in spite of labor on this
stylized conception am glad I did it – time not wasted – learned a
lot – stylized solil. uncovered new insights into characters and
recurrent themes – job now is to get all this in naturally in straight
dialogue – as simple and direct and dynamic as possible – with as
few words – stop doing things to these characters – let them reveal
themselves – in spite of (or because of!) their long locked-up passions,
I feel them burning to do just this!
   Keep mask conception – but as Mannon *background*, not
foreground! – what I want from this mask concept is a dramatic
arresting visual symbol of the separateness, the fated isolation of
this family, the mark of their fate which makes them dramatically
distinct from rest of world – I see now how to retain this effect
without the use of built masks – by make-up – *in repose* (that is,
background) the Mannon faces are like life-like death masks – (death-
in-life motive, return to death-with-peace yearning that runs through
plays) – this can be gotten very effectively by make-up, as can also
the family resemblance – (make-up isn't a lost art in European
theatre, why should it be in ours? – only our shiftless inefficiency) –
I can visualize the death-mask-like expression of characters' faces
in repose suddenly being torn open by passion as extraordinarily

effective – moreover, its exact visual representation of what I want expressed –

Rewrite trilogy along these lines – and get more architectural fixed form into outer structure – and more composition (in musical sense) into inner structure – more definite recurrence of themes ('Island' death fear and death wish, the family past, etc.) – always bearing in mind – Mannon drama takes place on a plane where outer reality is mask of true fated reality – unreal realism –

Make into even more definite fixed pattern superficial characteristic type realism of the chorus of the town (the world outside which always sees without really seeing or understanding) and the simple healthy normality – goodness – of Hazel and Peter.

Repetition of the same scene – in its essential spirit, sometimes even in its exact words, but between different characters – following plays as development of fate – theme demands this repetition – Mannon & Christine (about Brant) in 1st play, Christine & Orin (about Brant) in second play – Mannon & Christine in 4th act, 1st play, Lavinia & Orin in 2nd act, 3rd play – etc.

25.   23 September 1930 (Le Plessis)
Start rewriting.

26.   15 October 1930 (Le Plessis)
Finish rewriting – off for a trip to Spain and Morocco.

27.   19 November 1930 (Le Plessis)
Read last version – fairly well satisfied – got right line to it, at least – and quality I want – but needs considerable work yet – several new ideas I want to try out – may bring added value – not sure – only way try and see – start on this at once.

28.   10 January 1931 (Paris)
Have finished most of new stuff – getting plays typed as I work –

29.   2 February 1931 (Paris)
Typing finished with all new stuff in – let it rest now –

30.   7 February 1931 (Le Plessis)
Read over – don't like most of new stuff – all right but introduces too many added complications – trying to get added values has blurred those I had – too much of muchness – would need another play added to do it right – and would be wrong even then! – can't crowd intuitions all hidden aspects of life form into one work! – I

better throw most of this new stuff out – some valuable and can be condensed and retained – but in general revert entirely to former version.

31.   20 February 1931 (Le Plessis)
Revision finished – off to Canary islands for a sun and sea vacation –

32.   8 March 1931 (Las Palmas, Canary Islands)
Read typed script – looks damned good to me – funny how typed pages bring out clearly values that too-long familiarity with longhand had rendered vague and undynamic – but plenty of work to do – no vacation here – script much too long, of course – needs cutting and condensing throughout – must rewrite end of 'The Hunted' – weak now – Christine's talk to Lavinia toward end bad stuff – first scene of Act One 'The Haunted' also needs rewriting and pointing up – flabby and faltering as now written – ends of Scenes One & Two 'The Hunted' also need work –

33.   26 March 1931 (Las Palmas)
Finished work – return to France (Marseilles) Casablanca and Tangier tomorrow – script retyped –

34.   4 April 1931 (Paris)
Decide change Scenes One & Two, Act One, 'The Hunted' to Acts One & Two – they are properly acts, not scenes – but Scene One Act One of 'The Haunted' is properly a scene – question of feeling, this! – no rules about it –

35.   9 April 1931 (Paris)
New script retyped – copies off to Guild [Theatre] –

36.   August 1931 (Northport, Long Island), N.Y.
Read over galley proofs from Liveright – after nearly four months of not looking at this trilogy, get fairly fresh impact – moved by it – has power and drive and the strange quality of unreal reality I wanted – main purpose seems to me soundly achieved – there is a feeling of fate in it, or I am a fool – a psychological modern approximation of the fate in the Greek tragedies on this theme – attained without benefit of supernatural –

   And technically (although this is of minor importance, naturally) I flatter myself it is unique thing in dramaturgy – each play complete episode completely realized but at same time, which is the important point, not complete in that its end begins following play and demands that play as an inevitable sequel – few trilogies in existence in drama of all time and none of them has this quality which, in any time under any conditions, could not have failed to prove an asset – if gained without harm to the separate play, of course, as I believe I have done.

('Interlude' never got credit for this technical virtue – without which its successful production would have been impossible – that the first part rounded out a complete section of Nina's life with a definite beginning and end and yet contained the suspense at its end which called for Part Two – otherwise dinner interval would have wrecked it – no other two-part play, as far as I know, has accomplished this synthesis of end and beginning –)

37. August 1931 (Northport)
Work on galley proofs – cutting is needed, especially in first and third plays –

38. September 1931 (Northport)
Work on second galleys – several points strike me – work I did at Canary Islands was of great value in most of results – but feel now a few things eliminated there should be restored – Lavinia's last appeal to Peter near very end – some things in Act Two which help to clear it up – this Act Two of 'The Haunted' is weak spot still – needs rearranging – but will postpone final decision on this until I hear cast read plays – then it will hit my ear.

SOURCE: extracts from 'Working Notes and Extracts from a Fragmentary Work Diary', first published as 'O'Neill's Own Story of *Electra* in the Making', *New York Herald Tribune* (3 Nov. 1931); reproduced in Barrett H. Clark (ed.), *European Theories of the Drama* (New York, 1947), pp. 530–6. A photo-copy of the original MS was included in the 'special edition' of the *Electra* trilogy produced by Horace Liveright Inc. (New York, 1931).

2. COMMENTATORS ON THE 1931 PRODUCTION

Stark Young   (1931)

'Classic suspense . . . most modern of his plays'

To hear the bare story, shortly told, of this new O'Neill play, with all its crimes and murders, may easily bring a flouting smile or recall Mrs Malaprop's announcement of Sir Lucius's and Bob Acres's duel: 'So, so, here's fine work, here's fine suicide, parricide, and simulation going on in the fields!' The same thing could be said of *Hamlet* or *King Lear* or *Oedipus King*, of course, but this is sure to be the line the jibes will take from such of the play's critics as are unfriendly or impatient or incapable. As to the length of the event, the actual performance at the Guild [Theatre] could be considerably shortened by going faster in many places – though, take it for all in all, the length of the play itself is for the most part organic with both its meaning and its effect. As to its depressing effects, we will come to that later.

The title, as we see, intends to dispose at the start of the relation of *Mourning Becomes Electra* to the Greek drama. The story of the house of Atreus was set down by Homer, Pindar, Aeschylus, Sophocles, Euripides and divers other Greek writers whose words are not extant. From this house shadowed by an ancient curse, Agamemnon, brother of Menelaus, goes forth to the war at Troy. His wife Clytaemnestra, the sister of Helen, during her husband's absence takes for her paramour Aegisthos and shares the government of Argos with him. In due time Agamemnon, having at the god's behest sacrificed his daughter Iphigenia and bringing with him Cassandra, Priam's daughter, returns, and is murdered by Clytaemnestra and her lover. Electra, his daughter, is shamed and degraded and prays for the return of her brother Orestes, long ago sent out of the country by his mother and now become a man. Orestes returns, kills Clytaemnestra and Aegisthos. He is pursued by the Erinnyes, and only after wandering and agony and a vindication of himself before the tribunal of Athena's Areopagos is he cleansed of his sin.

Mourning Becomes Electra begins with the mother and daughter, Christine and Lavina, waiting, there in this house of the Mannons, the return of Ezra Mannon from the war, which with Lee's surrender is about over. A thread of romance is introduced between Lavinia and Peter, and between Lavinia's brother, Orin, and Hazel, Peter's sister. Meanwhile Captain Brant comes to call; he pays a certain court to Lavinia, and she, acting on a cue from the hired man, who has been on the place these sixty years, traps him into admitting that he is the son of one of the Mannons who had seduced a Canadian maid-servant and been driven from home by his father, Lavinia's grandfather. She has all her data straight now. She has suspected her mother, followed her to New York, where Christine has pretended to go because of her own father's illness, but has in fact been meeting Adam Brant. Lavinia has written her father and her brother, hinting at the town gossip about her mother. We learn that Captain Brant had returned to avenge his mother but instead had fallen passionately in love with Christine, who loves him as passionately as she hates her husband. From this point the play moves on, with the father's hatred of the son, who returns it, the son's adoration of his mother, the daughter's and the mother's antagonism, the daughter's and father's devotion, to Christine's murder of her husband with the poison sent by Brant and substituted for the medicine prescribed against his heart trouble. Part One of the play ends here. Orin returns, after an illness from a wound in the head. Christine tries to protect herself in her son's mind against the plots of Lavinia. Lavinia, in the room where her father's body lies, convinces him with the facts; they trail Christine to Brant's ship, where she has gone to warn him against Orin. Orin shoots Brant. Christine next day kills herself. Brother and sister take a long voyage to China, stop at the southern isles, come home again. Substitutions have taken place, Lavinia has grown like her mother, Orin more like his father. Meanwhile his old affair with Hazel, encouraged at last by Lavinia, who now wants to marry Peter, is cancelled; he finds himself making an incestuous proposal to Lavinia and is repulsed by her. He shoots himself. In the end Lavinia, speaking words of love to Peter, finds Adam's name on her lips. She breaks with Peter, orders the blinds of her house nailed shut, and goes into the house, to live there till her death. Justice has been done, the Mannon dead will be there and she will be there.

So bare an account serves the plot a little, but can give scant indication of the direct speeches and actions heavily charged with the burden and meaning of the scenes; nor does it convey the power and direct arrangement of some of them – that, for example, of the brother and sister at Brant's cabin, where the mere visual elements convey as much as the words. The chanty with which this scene opens, the song and the singer's drunkenness, the lonely ship in the dusk, establishing as it does the mood of longing, futility, land-chains and the sea's invitation and memory, is a fine idea and greatly enriches the texture of the play.

It will be obvious that the American dramatist, as the Greek did, used a well known outline which he could fill in to his purpose. Obviously, too, Ezra Mannon is Agamemnon, Captain Brant Aegisthos, Christine Clytaemnestra, Lavinia Electra, and Orin Orestes. But to dismiss the matter by saying that Mr O'Neill has merely repeated the classic story in modern terms is off the track. Let it go at that and you will miss even the really classic elements in the play and get only the Greek side of it that is self-evident and that would be easy for any dramatist to imitate.

The story itself follows the Greeks up to the middle of the third division of the play, and here the incest motive, the death of Orin and the transference of the whole situation and dramatic conclusion from the mother to the sister depart from Aeschylus, Sophocles and Euripides. Adam Brant's relation to the family adds to the rôle of the lover the motif of a blood relationship. The old hired man, the confidant, parallels to some extent a Greek device, familiar to us in countless plays. The townspeople and workmen are now and again a kind of chorus. Many of the shadings and themes are from the older plays; for a good example, the servant's line in Aeschylus about the dead killing one who lives, which underlies one of the new play's main themes. The death of the lover, as in Aeschylus and Euripides, not as in Sophocles, comes before that of the mother, which throws the stress where the O'Neill play needs it. The division of the play into three parts is, of course, like the trilogy of the Greek dramatists. On the other hand, the dividing line is much less distinct in *Mourning Becomes Electra*; the final curtain of the first part, for example, falls, it is true, on Mannon's death, as in Aeschylus it does on Agamemnon's, but there is not the same effect of totality because of the stress put on Lavinia; in *Agamemnon* Electra does not even appear.

The magnificent theme that there is something in the dead that we cannot placate falsely is in the Greek plays and in the O'Neill play. The end of the play is by imaginative insight Greek in spirit: Lavinia goes into the house, the blinds are closed forever, the stage is silent, the door shut, the exaltation is there, the completion, the tragic certainty. Finally, the peculiar kind of suspense employed in the play is Greek. The playwright has learned the adult suspense of the classics as compared with the adolescent concept of suspense, hit off happily enough at times, that reigns in the romantic drama of the North. Classic suspense does not depend on a mere crude strain, wondering how things will turn out, however entertaining and often dramatic that effect may be. The classic suspense has even a biological defence: you know that in life you will come to death, but just how the course of all your living will shade and fulfill itself you do not know, and you are borne up by an animal will to survive, a passionate participation, an absorbed contemplation of the course to be run, till the last moment completes itself. In the classic form, where the outcome is already known, lies the highest order of suspense. Knowing how things will end, you are left free to watch what qualities and what light will appear in their progression toward their due and necessary finish. You hang on what development, what procession exactly of logic, ecstasy or fate, will ensue with them, what threads of beautiful or dark will come into their human fabric. Suspense proves thus to be not necessarily a contrivance, effective as that may be; it is an inner quality.

It is interesting in our confused and feministic epoch that this new employment of the theme gives the play to Electra. Nowhere in Greek does this happen. From Sophocles there survives what must be only a section of a trilogy, the *Electra*; and though so much of the torment and waiting has been hers, Electra is at the end let off with a betrothal to Orestes's faithful Horatio, Pylades, and the forebodings and remorse rise in Orestes only, who has struck the death blow on his mother. In Euripides's *Electra* the conclusion is the forebodings of Orestes and the marriage of Electra to Pylades; in his *Orestes* Electra cleaves to her brother, who is in a violent neurotic sickness, quite modernly indicated; they are both in danger from the State for their action, and the whole situation is solved with a trivial and silly dénouement, gods from the machine, killings and abductions, wholly undramatic and redeemed, in so far as it is redeemed, only by Euripides's dialectic and poetic glamor. In Aeschylus, Electra appears only in the middle of the trilogy; the central hero is the royal line, represented by Agamemnon and Orestes.

Along with these more accessible and manifest likes and dislikes, there are numerous points about Mr O'Neill's play that are additions to or changes from the original Greek and that are yet both high creative invention and, in modern terms and material, re-creations in the most profound sense of Greek equivalents. The most brilliant of these is the incest motive, coming toward the last of the play. (We must recall Shelley's remark that, of all tragic motives, incest is the most powerful, since it brings the passions most violently into play.) For Orestes the gray forms at the back, invisible at first to all but himself, are the Erinyes, the Furies who will avenge the crime he has committed within his own blood. They are the daughters of night, and when they have been appeased, their other selves, the Eumenides, the Gentle Ones, will pass by and leave him peace. For Orin Mannon there comes the sudden form of his desire; Incest: the realisation and admission of what it has all been about all along, his feelings toward his father, toward his mother, toward Brant, toward Lavinia. This recognition of his obsession is his avenging Erinyes. In this detail alone might rest the argument that Eugene O'Neill, placing a Greek theme in the middle of the last century, has written the most modern of all his plays.

The motive of the resemblance among the three men, Mannon, Orin and Brant, is a great dramatic image: it proves a parallel to the Greek motive of a cursed house, and at the same time remains modern and fresh. The Greek husband returned from the war with his paramour and after sacrificing his daughter; Mannon's return will bring the son also home again, to a more subtle and complex situation than the other. The Islands of the Blest, everywhere in Greek dreams, the southern islands that are the symbol of so much modern meaning in *Mourning Becomes Electra*, make a fine motif. The mother in *Mourning Becomes Electra* is not killed by her son but takes her own life; his essential murder, nevertheless, of his mother turns in his mind with a terror more modern but no less destroying; his mind storms with the Furies – 'thoughts that accuse each other', as Cicero, writing in the sophistication of four centuries after Sophocles, defined them.

It is not the Guild's fault if there is no overwhelming performance in *Mourning Becomes Electra*. The casting of such a play is very difficult, and doubly so in the absence of any training in our theatre that would prepare actors for the requirements of such parts. The best performances came in the scenes between the mother and son, where Mme Nazimova's sense of theatre and her fluid response combined with Mr Earle Larimore's simple and right attack on his rôle, were truly convincing, and in the scene between husband and wife, where Mr Lee Baker gave a wholly right impersonation and the exact dramatic value for the play. Mr Erskine Sanford turns out admirably in two character parts, the village doctor and the old workman who takes a bet on braving the ghost in the house. Miss Alice Brady had the rôle of all rôles in the play most difficult. Her performance of this modern Electra was sincere, and was sustained at times not only by a sort of *tour-de-force* achievement, but with real physical power, voice and all. In a few scenes she was pathetic as well, clear and moving, and her beauty most impressive. No doubt there was some instruction from the author himself as to keeping the face like a mask, rigid and motionless, as if fate itself were living there in this passionate and resolute being. As for the Greek of that intention, we must recall that in the Attic theatre the mask for Electra was very likely one of tortured lines, that the Greek theatre changed masks if need be from one scene to another, and that the Greek actor in the part could avail himself of gesture, dance movement and a thorough training in voice, metre, speech and singing. Realistically, which is to say, in life, such rigidity never occurs except as a sign of disease. Aesthetically it belongs only in the midst of a general stylistic whole, as in the Greek drama or the Chinese theatre that Mei Lan-fang brought to us. Technically it is immensely difficult, and derives not from an actual rigidity at all. Rigidity, mask-like to the utmost, if you will, is a form of rhythm, as silence, when perceptible, exists within a rhythm. It is unfair to bring so great an artist as Mei Lan-fang into the argument, but he gave us the whole model for such a problem in acting – the eyes constantly moving, the head imperceptibly in motion, supported by a complete and often almost invisible rhythm of the body, the emotions precise and compelling because of their very abstraction. Miss Brady's performance had several unforgettable moments. On the whole it moved gravely and in a manner remarkably well sustained just below the surface of the motives set for her by the dramatist; but her performance, by failing both the darkness and the exaltation of the part, often made only oppressive and unvaried what should have been burning and unconquerably alive and dominating. When we come right down to it, however, the best acting in the play is Mr Earle Larimore's. In all his scenes up to the very last part, where he mouths too much and makes faces instead of a more intense concentration on his effects, he is excellent. In the scenes with his mother especially, he contrived by a certain emotional humility before the moment in which he shared to come out securely right.

Out of Mr Robert Edmond Jones's curtain and four settings, the rooms and the ship seem to me adequate without any haunting of the imagination, the front of the house dramatically right save for the lighting toward the rear, unnecessarily cruel to the actors. Mr Philip Moeller's directing was admirable all through for its taste and evenness, its clear movement and fine placing of the scene. Its one fault was its tempo. There can be no doubt that Mr O'Neill's play suffers greatly and will be accused of pretentiousness where it is wholly sincere and direct, because of the slowness with which the speeches are said. Very often the effect is only that of a bourgeois respect for something to be taken as important. If it is the Greek spirit that is sought, the answer is that the Greek reading of lines was certainly formal but not necessarily slow; the chances are, in fact, that in the Greek theatre the cues were taken closely in order to keep the music going. And the Greeks had the advantage of music, dancing and a great declamatory style, the lack of which will have to be balanced by anything rather than this obvious spacing and pausing and frequent monotone that we encounter at the Guild.

In *Mourning Becomes Electra* Mr O'Neill comes now into the full stretch of clear narrative design. He discovers that in expressive pattern lies the possibility of all that parallels life, a form on which fall infinite shadings and details, as the light with its inexhaustible nuances and elements appears on a wall. He has come to what is so rare in Northern art, an understanding of the depth and subtlety that lie in repetition and variation on the same design.

As to the depressing element of *Mourning Becomes Electra*, I have only to say that it seems to me above anything else exhilarating. There is a line of Leopardi's where he speaks of poetry as 'my delight and my Erinyes'; and once, thinking of the eternal silence, he hears the wind among the trees and goes comparing the infinite silence to that voice, and remembers the eternal, and the dead seasons, and the present and living, and the sound of it, *e il suon di lei*. In this immensity his thought drowns, and shipwreck is sweet to him in such a sea. When the play ended, and the last Mannon was gone into the house, the door shut, I felt in a full, lovely sense that the Erinyes were appeased, and that the Eumenides, the Gentle Ones, passed over the stage.

SOURCE: review ('Eugene O'Neill's New Play') of the opening perform- ance, 26 October 1931, in *New Republic* (11 Nov. 1931); reproduced in Young's *Immortal Shadows* (New York, 1948), pp. 132–9.

John Mason Brown   (1931)

'Tragic Melodrama of Heroic Proportions'

For exciting proof that the theatre is still very much alive, that it still has grandeur and ecstasy to offer to its patrons, that fine acting has not disappeared from behind the footlights' glare, that productions which thrill with memorability are still being made, that scenic design and stage direction can belong among the fine arts, and that the Theatre Guild, in spite of any causes for discouragement it may have given in the past, is still the most accomplished as well as the most intrepid producing organisation in America, you have only to journey to the Guild Theatre these nights and days, and sit before Eugene O'Neill's new trilogy, *Mourning Becomes Electra*. It is a play which towers above the scrubby output of our present-day theatre as the Empire State Building soars above the skyline of Manhattan. Most of its fourteen acts, and particularly its earlier and middle sections, are possessed of a strength and majesty equal to its scale. It boasts, too, the kind of radiant austerity which was part of the glory that was Greece.

It is one of the most distinguished achievements of Mr O'Neill's career. It is – as the dull word has it – uneven; but so (as the no less dull retort phrases it) are the Himalayas. It has blemishes which are obvious, especially as it reaches its third section. But it remains to the end a *magnum opus* besides which *Strange Interlude* and most of the earlier, simpler plays sink into unimportance. For it is an experiment in sheer, shuddering, straightforward story-telling which widens the theatre's limited horizons at the same time it is exalting and horrifying its patrons.

It retells, as everyone knows, a story of revenge; a saga of the way in which fate calls upon Electra and her brother Orestes to avenge the murder of their father, Agamemnon, by slaying their wicked mother, Clytemnestra, and her no less wicked lover, Aegisthus. It is a myth all three of the great tragic dramatists of Greece have told in their own way, taking their own liberties with its details, distributing the emphasis according to their own sensing of its moral and dramatic values, and managing to make it decidedly their own in each of their independent versions. Mr O'Neill, needless to say, has taken even greater liberties with this classic myth than any of his ancient predecessors dared to do. By taking them, he has made the story very much his own, without robbing its terrible sequence of catastrophes of either their force or their essential outlines.

The play finds Mr O'Neill forgetting the pseudo-scientific jargon of Mother Dynamo and the mystic laugh of Lazarus,[1] dispensing with such special technical devises as masks and asides, and writing without any hindrances of form as an emotionalist. As an emotionalist, who knows how to dramatise the curdling rancors of hate, the surgings of thwarted passion, and the taut demands of murder, he has no equal in the contemporary theatre. As his title makes very clear, Mr O'Neill's concern is with one of the grandest, most spine-twisting tales of murder the theatre's history knows. It is, in short, the Electra story he is retelling in more or less modern terms, substituting the white pillars of a country house in Civil War New England for the Doric columns of ancient Argos.

Mr O'Neill's play is a testing of his strength with that fable of the luckless house of Atreus which Aeschylus first treated in the *Oresteia*, which Sophocles and Euripides both dealt with in their respective *Electras*, and which such a modern as the late Hugo von Hofmannsthal vulgarised into a Reinhardtian thriller of lights and leers and snakelike gestures. Unlike Sophocles and Euripides, who contented themselves with the writing of a single play about the 'recognition' of the long-separated Electra and Orestes, and the murder of Clytemnestra and Aegisthus, Mr O'Neill has turned to Aeschylus for the model of *Mourning Becomes Electra*. Like this earliest of the Greek tragic writers, he has chosen to give the story in full, to prepare for its coming, to catch it at the height of its action, and to follow his avengers (he follows both Electra and Orestes) past the awful deed fate has demanded of them to the time when the Erinyes (or Furies) are pursing them. Accordingly, just as Aeschylus divided his *Oresteia* into the *Agamemnon*, *The Choëphori*, or *Libation Bearers*, and *The Eumenides*, so Mr O'Neill has divided his *Mourning Becomes Electra* into three parts bearing such Bulwer-Lytton titles as *Homecoming*, *The Hunted* and *The Haunted*. Contrary to the example of Aeschylus, and much more according to the practice of Sophocles and Euripides, Mr O'Neill gives his trilogy to Electra. It is she who dominates its action and fuses it, even as Orestes fused the Aeschylean original into one long play – with pauses – rather than three separate dramas.

Mr O'Neill's Agamemnon (Lee Baker) is Ezra Mannon, a hard, unbending New Englander, who has been off to the Mexican War in his youth, who has studied law, been a skipper, achieved great success in business, and served as mayor of the small town in which his family is outstanding. His Clytemnestra (Alla Nazimova) is Christine, a foreigner who has long been out of love with her husband and who has now come to hate him. Their children, Lavinia (Alice Brady) and Orin (Earle Larimore), are, of course, the Electra and the Orestes of Mr O'Neill's piece. While old Ezra Mannon had been away from home, winning the praise of General Grant for the military abilities he has shown as a brigadier general in the Civil War, his wife has had an affair with a Captain Adam Brant (Thomas Chalmers), the Aegisthus of *Mourning Becomes Electra*, who in this case is the illegitimate son of a wayward Mannon who has brought shame on his family.

Lavinia, who has also been in love with Captain Brant, follows her mother to New York, learns of her infidelity to her father, and resolves to break up the affair. She confronts her mother, makes her promise to see no more of Brant, and prepares to welcome her father and brother home from the war. Meanwhile Christine has already confided in Brant that their own way to happiness lies in the death of Ezra, who stands between them. She is prepared to murder him, and murder him she does by taking advantage of the heart trouble from which he suffers. Not only does she bring on one of his attacks by naming her lover to him but she offers him as a medicine the poison Brant has sent her. Lavinia comes into her father's room just before he dies, hears him accuse her mother, sees the powder she has administered, and resolves to take justice into her own hands in avenging his death.

Both Lavinia and her mother fight for the love of Orin, but he, like the spineless Orestes of Sophocles and Euripides, soon falls under the domination of Lavinia. She proves her point to him by leading him to the clipper ship Brant commands and there shows him their mother in Brant's arms. Thereupon Orin kills Brant when his mother has left him; she commits suicide when she learns of her lover's death (thus sparing us the mother-murder of the Greeks); the ghosts of the dead who refuse to die haunt Orin and Lavinia; Orin shoots himself; and Lavinia forswears the happiness her impending marriage might have brought her, has the shutters nailed down on the Mannon house, and locks herself inside it to atone during the rest of her life for the sins of her family.

As Mr O'Neill rehandles this venerable story it preserves its awesome fascination. It emerges, as it has always emerged, as one of the most gripping melodramatic plots in the world. It also comes through its present restatement as a tragic melodrama of heroic proportions. The poetic beauty the Greeks gave it is lacking in Mr O'Neill's prose modernisation. But the dilemma remains, and so does much of the agony and exaltation that belong to it. Mr O'Neill's treatment of it is vigorous with the kind of vigor our theatre rarely sees. It is stark, unadorned and strong. It has dignity and majesty. Nearly the whole of it is possessed of such an all-commanding interest that one is totally unconscious of the hours its performance freely consumes.

That it is longer than it need be seems fairly obvious, as does the fact that, like so many of O'Neill's plays, it stands in need of editing. It is at its best in its first two sections, and most particularly in its fine middle portion. But its last part seems overlong and lacks the interest of its predecessors. It marks the same falling off from what has preceded it as the *Eumenides* does from the *Choëphori*. Deprived of plotting which sweeps forward to a climax, and dealing with the conscience-stricken course of its avengers, it goes a tamer, more uncertain way. Nor is it helped by the incest motive Mr O'Neill has added. It rises in the last act, however, to a final curtain that is Greek in its whole feeling and flavor.

Alla Nazimova's Christine is superbly sinister, possessed of an insidious and electric malevolence, and brilliant with an incandescent fire. As Lavinia Miss [Alice] Brady gives the kind of performance her admirers have long been waiting to see her give. It is controlled. It has the force of the true Electra. And it is sustained throughout as long and severe an actor's test as any player has been called upon to meet. The moments when she stands dressed in black before the black depths of Mr [Robert Edmond] Jones's doorways are moments no one can forget who has felt their thrill. Mr [Earle] Larimore's Orin is a vivid picture of frenzy and weakness. All in all, *Mourning Becomes Electra* is an achievement which restores the theatre to its high estate.

SOURCE: review ('Eugene O'Neill's Exciting Trilogy Is Given an Excellent Production') of opening performance, 26 October 1931, in *New York Post* (27 Oct. 1931); reproduced in Brown's *Dramatis Personae* (New York, 1965), pp. 53–7.

NOTE

1. [Ed.] Mother Dynamo and Lazarus – references, respectively, to *Dynamo* (1928; produced 1929) and *Lazarus Laughed* (1926; produced 1928).

Brooks Atkinson   (1931)

'Universal Tragedy of Tremendous Stature'

Mr O'Neill gives not only size but weight in *Mourning Becomes Electra*, which the Theatre Guild mounted at its own theatre for the greater part of yesterday afternoon and evening. The size is a trilogy that consumes six hours in the playing. The weight is the formidable earnestness of Mr O'Neill's cheerless dramatic style. To him the curse that the fates have set against the New England house of Mannon is no trifling topic for a casual dramatic discussion, but a battering into the livid mysteries of life. Using a Greek legend as his model, he has reared up a universal tragedy of tremendous stature – deep, dark, solid, uncompromising and grim. It is heroically thought out and magnificently wrought in style and structure, and it is played by Alice Brady and Mme [Alla] Nazimova with consummate artistry and passion. Mr O'Neill has written overwhelming dramas in the past. In *Strange Interlude* [1928] he wrote one almost as long as this trilogy. But he has never before fulfilled himself so completely; he has never commanded his theme in all its variety and adumbrations with such superb strength, coolness and coherence. To this department, which ordinarily reserves its praise for the dead, *Mourning Becomes Electra* is Mr O'Neill's masterpiece.

As the title acknowledges, *Mourning Becomes Electra* follows the scheme of the Orestes-Electra legend which Aeschylus, Sophocles and Euripides translated into drama in the days of Greek classicism. Like the doomed house of Atreus, this New England family of Civil War time is dripping with foul and unnatural murder. The mother murders the father. The son murders his mother's lover. The mother mercifully commits suicide. The daughter's malefic importunities drive the son to suicide. It is a family that simmers with hatred, suspicion, jealousy and greed, and that is twisted by unnatural loves. Although Mr O'Neill uses the Orestes legend as the scheme of his trilogy, it is his ambition to abandon the gods, whom the Greeks humbly invoked at the crises of drama, and to interpret the whole legend in terms of modern psychology. From royalty this story of vengeance comes down to the level of solid New England burghers. From divinity it comes into the sphere of truths that are known. There are no mysteries about the inverted relationships that set all these gaunt-minded people against one another, aside from the primary mystery of the ferocity of life. Students of the new psychology will find convenient labels to explain why the mother betrays her husband, why the daughter instinctively takes the father's side, why the son fears his father and clings to his mother, why the daughter gradually inherits the characteristics of her mother after the deaths of the parents, and why the son transfers his passion to his sister. As for Mr O'Neill, he has been chiefly concerned with the prodigious task of writing these modern plays.

And through three plays and fifteen scenes he has kept the rhythm of his story sculptural in its stark outline. The Mannon curse is inherited. For this fine New England mansion was built in hatred when the Mannons cast off the brother who had sinned with a French-Canadian servant. Her son, Captain Brant, comes back into their lives to avenge his mother's dishonor and he becomes the lover of Ezra Mannon's wife. From that point on *Mourning Becomes Electra* stretches out as a strong chain of murders and revenge and the house of Mannon is a little island walled round with the dead.

There are big scenes all the way through. Before the first play is fairly started the dance of death begins with Lavinia upbraiding Christine, her mother, with secret adultery. Christine plotting with Captain Brant to poison her husband on the night when he returns from the Civil War; Christine poisoning her husband and being discovered with the tablets by Lavinia as the climax to the first play; Lavinia proving her mother's guilt to Orin, her brother, by planting the box of poison tablets on the breast of her dead father and admitting her terrified mother to the chamber of death; Lavinia and Orin following their mother to a rendezvous with the captain on his ship and murdering him in his cabin; Lavinia forcing her brother to suicide and waiting panic-stricken for the report of his pistol; Lavinia in the last scene of the last play sealing herself up with this haunted house to live with the spectres of her dead – all these are scenes of foreboding and horror.

Yet *Mourning Becomes Electra* is no parade of bravura scenes. For this is an organic play in which story rises out of character and character rises out of story, and each episode is foreshadowed by what precedes it. Although Mr O'Neill has been no slave to the classic origins of his tragedy, he has transmuted the same impersonal forces into the modern idiom, and the production, which has been brilliantly directed by Philip Moeller, gives you some of the stately spectacle of Greek classicism. Lavinia in a flowing black dress sitting majestically on the steps of Robert Edmond Jones's set of a New England mansion is an unforgettable and portentous picture. Captain Brant pacing the deck of his ship in the ringing silence of the night, the murdered Mannon lying on his bier in the deep shadows of his study, the entrances and exits of Christine and Lavinia through doors that open and close on death are scenes full of dramatic beauty. To give you perspective on this tragedy Mr O'Neill has a sort of Greek chorus in Seth, the hired man, and the frightened townsfolk who gather outside the house, laughing and muttering. He has viewed his tragedy from every side, and thought it through to the last detail and composed it in a straightforward dialogue that tells its story without hysteria.

As Mr O'Neill has mastered his play, so the actors have mastered their parts and so Mr Moeller has moulded the parts into a measured, fluent performance. Miss Alice Brady, as Lavinia, has one of the longest parts ever written. None of her neurotic dramatics in the past has prepared us for the demoniac splendor of her Lavinia.

She speaks in an ominous, full voice that only once or twice breaks into the splintery diffusion or artificial climaxes. Lavinia has recreated Miss Brady into a majestic actress. As Christine, Mme Alla Nazimova gives a performance of haunting beauty, rich in variety, plastic, eloquent and imaginatively transcendent. Lee Baker as the Mannon father conveys little of the towering indomitability of that part and lets his death scene crumple into mediocrity. Earle Larimore plays Orin from the inside with great resource, elasticity and understanding. As Captain Brant, Thomas Chalmers has a solid body to his playing. There are excellently designed bits by Arthur Hughes and Erskine Sanford as townspeople. Philip Foster, and especially Mary Arbenz, give able performances as a brother and sister.

For Mr O'Neill, for the Guild and for lovers of drama, *Mourning Becomes Electra* is, accordingly, an occasion for great rejoicing. Mr O'Neill has set his hand to a tremendous story, and told it with coolness and clarity. In sustained thought and workmanship it is his finest tragedy. All that he fretted over in the past has trained him for this masterpiece.

SOURCE: review ('Strange Images of Death in Eugene O'Neill's Masterpiece') of opening performance, 26 October 1931, in the *New York Times* (27 Oct. 1931).

Robert Benchley   (1931)

'Good, Old-Fashioned, Spine-Curling Melodrama'

In the midst of the acclaim with which Eugene O'Neill is being so justly hailed for his latest and most gigantic *tour-de-force*, *Mourning Becomes Electra*, and in the confusion of cross-references to the Greek dramatists from whom he derived his grim and overpowering story, are we not forgetting one very important source of his inspiration, without which he might perhaps have been just a builder of word-mountains? Was there not standing in the wings of the Guild Theatre, on that momentous opening night, the ghost of an old actor in a white wig, with drawn sword, who looked on proudly as the titanic drama unfolded itself, scene by scene, and who murmured, with perhaps just the suggestion of a chuckle: 'That's good, son! Give 'em the old Theatre!'? The actor I refer to needs no introduction to the older boys and girls here tonight – Mr James O'Neill, 'The Count of Monte Cristo' and the father of our present hero.

Let us stop all this scowling talk about 'the inevitability of the Greek tragedy' and 'O'Neill's masterly grasp of the eternal verities' and let us admit that the reason why we sat for six hours straining to hear each line through the ten-watt acoustics of the Guild Theatre was because *Mourning Becomes Electra* is filled with good, old-fashioned, spine-curling melodrama. It is his precious inheritance from his trouper-father, his father who counted 'One', 'Two', 'Three' as he destroyed his respective victims, one at the curtain to each act; it is his supreme sense of the Theatre in its most elementary appeal, which allows Eugene O'Neill to stand us on our heads (perhaps our heads would have been more comfortable) and keep us there from five in the afternoon until almost midnight. In this tremendous play he gives us not one thing that is new, and he gives us nothing to think about (unless we are just beginning to think), but he does thrill the bejeezus out of us, just as his father used to, and that is what we go to the theatre for.

Just run over in your mind the big scenes in *Mourning Becomes Electra*. A daughter upbraiding her mother for adultery, the mother plotting with her lover the murder of her husband, the poisoning of the husband and the discovery of the tablets in the fainting mother's hand, the placing of the tablets on the breast of the corpse to frighten the mother into a confession (and what a scene *that* was!), the brother and sister peering down the hatch of a sailing ship to spy on the mother and later to murder her lover, and the tense moments of waiting for the off-stage shots which would tell of the successive suicides of the mother and the brother. Greek tragedy, my eye! The idea may have been the Greeks', but the hand is the hand of Monte Cristo. If the Greek idea of revenge, murder, incest and suicide is so thrilling, why isn't Margaret Anglin busier than she is? *Mourning Becomes Electra* is just the old Greek story put into not particularly convincing New England talk, but it is a hundred times better show than *Electra* because O'Neill has a God-given inheritance of melodramatic sense. So let's stop kidding ourselves about the Verities and the Unities and take a grand, stupendous thriller when we find it and let it go at that.

In the face of such an overwhelming victory over Time, Space and the Daily Press as that which Mr O'Neill has won, it is perhaps puny in a single commentator to admit such a personal reaction as fatigue during the last of the three sections of the drama (for they are *not* three plays, as advertised, but one play in fourteen successive acts). But, willing as the spirit may be to take punishment, the human frame is not equipped for such a session as that which is imposed upon it in the Guild Theatre (at any rate, mine isn't, and I have a pretty good equipment), and, starting with a pretty bad scene (go ahead, strike me dead, Jove!) of comic relief at the beginning of the section called *The Haunted*, I began to be cushion-conscious. This uneasiness was heightened as I saw approaching that margin of Diminishing Returns in Tragedy which I alone seem to be conscious of in O'Neill's dramas, when one more fell swoop of Fate, one more killing, one more father in love with one more daughter, or one more sister in love with one more brother, and the whole thing becomes just a bit ridiculous. It was when I saw those magnificent scenes of the middle section becoming confused with a grand finale of bad comedy, incest and extra suicide that Miss Brady's agonised cry, 'I couldn't bear another death!', struck home, and I began to realise that, for me personally, *Mourning Becomes Electra* was getting to be just about one hour too long. I know that this is a purely individual and unworthy reaction, quite out of place in what should be a serious review of a great masterpiece, but, as this page is nothing if not personal, I am setting it down. And the final scene of all, in which Electra, or Lavinia, closes herself up in the great New England Greek temple for the rest of her unhappy life, content that mourning is her *métier*, made up for everything.

And now we come to Miss Brady and to Alla Nazimova and to all the rest of the splendid cast which the Theatre Guild has assembled to do homage to Mr O'Neill's *magnum opus*. Without them, and without Robert Edmond Jones's superb settings, I am not so sure just how effective the drama would be. I can imagine its being pretty bad, as a matter of fact, if only moderately well done. We thrill to the scenes between the mother and daughter on the steps of the old New England mansion, but how much credit do we give to Mr Jones and to Mr Moeller, who gave us this picture of two women in black on the white steps of a Greek temple? (It may have been so nominated in the 'script, but without Mr Jones to give it being, it might have remained just a stage-direction.) Alice Brady has at last come into her own, in voice and bearing the perfect Electra, and Nazimova, in spite of her Russian accent, which rings so strangely in Suffolk County, made so much of the sinning Clytemnestra that the drama lost much when she withdrew into the shades of the House of Mannon never to return. Earle Larimore, too, as Orin–Orestes, gave the rôle a human quality which could hardly have been expected in the writing, and Thomas Chalmers, with an opera-trained speaking voice, not only overcame the trick sound-currents of the theatre but gave a healthy robustness to the rather murky proceedings which was reassuring, as long as it lasted. Lee Baker, the first of a long string of entries to die, may have seemed a little stiff, but I suspect that it was a rather stiff part. In short, Philip Moeller in his direction, and the cast in their interpretation, and especially Mr Jones in his settings, all did more than their share to raise Mr O'Neill to the undisputed, and probably for a long time uncontested, eminence of the First Dramatist of Our Time. Not that he wasn't there already, but it is good to be sure.

But while we are on our feet, let us drink once again to the Count of Monte Cristo.

SOURCE: review of original production, in *The New Yorker* (7 Nov. 1931), pp. 28–30.

3. CRITICAL STUDIES

Normand Berlin   'Death and Determinism'
(1982)

According to an entry in his working diary, O'Neill finished the first draft of *Mourning Becomes Electra* on 21 February 1930. He began writing that draft in September 1929, one month before the stock market crash of October 1929. For many, that crash began the thirties in America, the time of the Depression, when millions became unemployed and hungry. The wild prosperous dreams of the 20s quickly vanished; the reality of soup-kitchens and pencil-selling took their place. 'Depression' is the word for an economic decline, but it also accurately describes the mood of a country that was once, only yesterday, the land of prosperity and opportunity, of Marco surnamed Millions, and was now the bitter land of dissatisfaction, of 'Brother, can you spare a dime?'. Hard times affect more than a nation's economics; the economic climate forces artists and intellectuals to seek causes and to express social concern. In the thirties many writers moved to the left, shouting out against a system that could produce the kind of poverty and general chaos that America was experiencing. The theatre of the thirties, its very existence threatened because of the loss of an audience, reflected the bitterness of the time, but it also generated an idealism connected with the desire to change the system. Outside of Broadway, politically active theatre groups began to form; they produced plays that were meant to engage new audiences and to spur them on to social action. The most important of these groups called itself the Group Theatre. An offshoot of the Theatre Guild, the company that produced O'Neill, this group – formed and guided by Harold Clurman, Cheryl Crawford, and Lee Strasberg – dedicated itself to performing plays that were critical of the American social system, and practised ensemble acting of the highest order. Their leading playwright was Clifford Odets, whose *Waiting for Lefty* (1935) made theatre history when its first audience left the performance with the word 'Strike!' ringing in the air. This 'happening' clearly indicates the social and political thrust of American theatre in the thirties, when most

playwrights addressed themselves to social protest – even revolutionary protest – and to the threat of fascism from Germany and Italy.
The nation seemed to be aflame with desire for change within and
with criticism of what was happening abroad – and the theatre held
a mirror to that flame.

America's leading dramatist, however, was stoking more personal
fires. While the other dramatists in their work faced the controversial
issues of the time, O'Neill was becoming more introspective. Always
interested in what was happening outside, in fact, deeply saddened
by the plight of the poor and the ominous rumblings of war, O'Neill
nevertheless avoided sociological attacks or propaganda in his plays
of the thirties and forties. Intensely private himself, O'Neill was
becoming more and more interested in private worlds, even if
they were found in universal myths. Working harder than ever,
ambitiously vying with the Greek dramatists for 'size' in drama, he
presents to the thirties of America *Mourning Becomes Electra* (written
1929–31, produced 1931), perhaps the best play of the thirties,
certainly the play possessing the greatest tragic depth, far different
from the plays that produced shouts of protest against hard times –
and more lasting.

In narrative line O'Neill's trilogy follows Aeschylus's *Oresteia*
rather closely in the first part (*The Homecoming*), somewhat closely
in the second part (*The Hunted*), rarely in the third part (*The Haunted*).
In *The Homecoming* the Mannon family (House of Atreus) awaits the
arrival of Ezra Mannon (Agamemnon) from the Civil War (Trojan
War) which has just concluded. His wife Christine (Clytemnestra)
has been having an affair with Adam Brant (Aegisthus), which
daughter Lavinia (Electra), who also loves Adam, has discovered.
(Adam Brant is the son of David Mannon and Marie Brantôme,
the Mannons' French servant, loved by the brothers David and Abe
Mannon, Ezra's father. The sexual seduction of Marie by David
causes a jealous and angry Abe to banish them from the polluted
house and to burn it down. Because of the harsh treatment of his
mother by the Mannons, Adam Brant – short for Brantôme – vows
revenge, but in the course of his scheme of revenge he falls in love
with Christine.) Lavinia, who hates her mother, tells Christine she
knows of the affair and makes Christine promise to break it off;
otherwise, Lavinia will tell her returning father, whom she adores.
Christine and Adam plan the murder of Ezra, who returns from the
war a changed man, softer, less Puritanical, genuinely seeking love
from his wife, trying (like Ephraim Cabot) to break down a wall
between himself and the wife who loathes him. Christine, in their
bedroom, informs Ezra of her affair with Adam, knowing that this

will affect his weak heart; when he asks for his medicine, she gives him poison. The play ends with Lavinia coming into the bedroom to see her father die as he points 'an accusing finger' at Christine. (This is only one of several melodramatic moments in the trilogy, O'Neill having learned much from his father's theatre.) Lavinia vows revenge. O'Neill, in *The Homecoming*, stays close to Aeschylus's story of the return of a war hero who is murdered by his wife and her paramour. O'Neill's treatment differs in the way the hero is killed (poison rather than a more direct slaying by Clytemnestra and Aegisthus), in the way the returning hero is portrayed (Ezra is more sympathetic if less heroic than Agamemnon, who sacrificed a daughter and who returns with a mistress), in the motive of Christine (whose hatred of her Puritanical husband stems from his making her feel 'disgust' in their love-making) and, most important, in the presentation of Lavinia (Electra does not appear in Aeschylus's *Agamemnon*).

In *The Hunted* Orin Mannon (Orestes) returns from the war, happy to be reunited with the mother he loves. Lavinia tells him about their mother's relationship with Adam Brant. Needing proof, Orin is taken by Lavinia to Adam's ship on a Boston wharf (the central scene of the trilogy), where he sees his mother with her lover. When Christine leaves, Orin kills Brant. Orin tells his mother what he has done, which causes Christine to commit suicide. The play ends with Orin hysterically accusing himself of having murdered his mother. In this play O'Neill's most important departure from Aeschylus is the suicide of Christine; in Aeschylus her son murders her. But the resulting pangs of conscience in the son remain the same – in Aeschylus the Furies, deploring matricide, appear on stage to torment Orestes; in O'Neill Orin's own thoughts cause him to break down. Also, in Aeschylus, the god Apollo, deploring the murder of Agamemnon, urges Orestes to avenge his father's death, whereas in O'Neill Electra serves that function. Although Electra does appear in Aeschylus's *The Libation Bearers*, her rôle in that play is much less important than Lavinia's role in *The Hunted*.

In *The Haunted*, which ends the trilogy, Lavinia and Orin return from a South Seas island vacation which was meant to help them forget the dreadful events of the past. Lavinia seems free; she has changed her customary black to her mother's green, has changed her hair style to her mother's, is more vivacious than ever before, in fact, now closely resembles Christine in every way. Orin, however, remains sick at heart and sick of mind. He is still plagued by his guilt in the death of his mother and, added to that, he has transferred his incestuous love for mother to an incestuous love for sister.

(Electra, now very much like Christine, is in fact playing the Mother to Orin, who now resembles his father Ezra, so that Electra is also playing the wife to her 'father', a role she yearned for while mother and father were alive.) Orin's declaration of his incestuous love for Lavinia causes her to reject him. Confronting his own twisted nature and his guilt, Orin commits suicide. Lavinia, ready for a happy life with Peter (who has loved her throughout the trilogy) and hoping that their love 'will drive the dead away', passionately says to him: 'Want me! Take me, Adam!' This Freudian slip causes her to realise that the dead cannot be driven away, that, in fact, her love for Adam Brant (who also resembled her father) was the reason for her hatred of her mother and for her revenge. She enters the Mannon house to face the ghosts of the past, and shuts the door behind her, as the curtain descends. In this play O'Neill leaves Aeschylus far behind. In *The Eumenides* Orestes is tormented by the Furies, is brought to trial for his matricide, and is absolved of his crime, with the Furies turning to goddesses of mercy. A positive ending, restoring balance and order to society, with passion turning to reason, dark to light. In *The Haunted* there is no absolution for Orin; death ends his agony. And there are no gods on stage, or anywhere else, to restore order. The darkness remains darkness. But, most important, Electra, who does not appear in *The Eumenides*, is the focus of O'Neill's attention; she takes centre-stage. She is the prime mover of the play's action; her final act is the memorable culmination of all her actions in the three plays, truly the 'tragic ending worthy of [her] character', to use the words in O'Neill's diary. The trilogy, as the title indicates, belongs to Lavinia.

O'Neill used the classical Electra story but made it his own, just as he used and made his own the Hippolytus legend in *Desire Under the Elms*. He changes much – easily pinpointed and too easily criticised by those who wish to demonstrate the superiority of the ancients – but he keeps what is essential to tragedy, death and determinism. Death is the trilogy's preoccupation. Mentioning the deaths that occur during the play's action – the murders of Ezra Mannon and Adam Brant, the suicides of Christine and Orin Mannon – points to the play's melodrama, but does not suggest the full impact of the idea of death. The trilogy's atmosphere is filled with the darkness of death. In exterior scenes, if the sun is not setting, then the moon is casting its eerie light – all scenes taking place in late afternoon or evening. In interior scenes, if candles are not flickering in dark rooms, then the lighted lamp is 'turned low'. The fading sunlight of the trilogy's beginning causes 'black bars of shadow' to fall on the gray wall from the white columns of the

Greek-style house, suggesting the cage that all the Mannons occupy. Forever fond of the circle, O'Neill repeats this effect in the last scene of the trilogy, at the end of which Lavinia literally enters the darkness of the cage.

Between Lavinia's first entrance from the house and her last exit into the house, death exerts insistent pressure on the trilogy. Its widest historical context is the Civil War. At his homecoming, Ezra Mannon reminds us of the death of Lincoln, and takes little joy in the victory of the North: 'All victory ends in the defeat of death.' Orin gives a graphic account of his 'heroic' deed of killing a man, and then killing another – 'It was like murdering the same man twice. I had a queer feeling that war meant murdering the same man over and over, and that in the end I would discover the man was myself.' Sometimes, he goes on to say, the face of that murdered man was his father's. Like war, Puritanism brings death, here death of the soul. Ezra, regretting his past mistakes in his relationship with Christine, tells her that Mannons 'went to the white meeting-house on Sabbaths and meditated on death. Life was a dying. Being born was starting to die. Death was being born.' Death occupies Ezra Mannon's study in the guise of portraits of the dead Mannons. The corpse of Ezra Mannon is *on stage* in Act Three of *The Hunted*, structurally the central act of the trilogy's thirteen acts. Orin, looking at his dead father, realises that 'Death becomes the Mannons.' The very next scene – the one that O'Neill in his diary pinpointed as the 'centre' of the trilogy (structurally it is the centre if we count separately the two scenes in Act One of *The Haunted*) – takes place on the stern of Adam Brant's clipper ship. Here, the only time we are away from the Mannon house, we are presented with the possibility of relief from 'the temple of death', as Ezra called it, perhaps the kind of relief Shakespeare affords in *Macbeth* when he moves his scene away from sick Scotland to an England that heals. But this is not the case. Immediately O'Neill brings death into the ship scene. An old chantyman sings 'Shenandoah' mournfully, and tells of the good old days, now gone forever. He reminds us of the previous scene with these words: 'Everything is dyin'! Abe Lincoln is dead. I used to ship on the Mannon packets an' I seed in the paper where Ezra Mannon was dead!' Then he sings 'Hanging Johnny'. Adam Brant's reaction: 'Damn that chanty! It's sad as death!' Of course, in this scene we will witness the on-stage murder of Brant who, as Orin discovers, looks like Ezra Mannon – 'I've killed him before – over and over.' To specify all the references to death and their contexts is to review the entire trilogy, so pervasive is the idea.

Death is tightly bound up with determinism because the ghosts of the dead not only haunt the living but also control their destinies. All of the events of the present are triggered by the Abe Mannon/Dave Mannon/Marie Brantôme triangle of the past. Here the curse on the House of Mannon is clearly mirroring the curse on the House of Atreus. The portraits of the dead Mannons hover over the play's action; the play's characters are in the cage formed by the shadows of the dead, and there is no escape. The past controls the present, as always in O'Neill.

Working along with the determinism connected with a family curse is the determinism based on psyche. This is the 'modern psychological approximation of Greek sense of fate'[1] that gave O'Neill his greatest challenge. For the most part, O'Neill is successful in weaving Freud into the fabric of his tragedy. The incestuous love of Orin for his mother and his sister, of Lavinia for her father, the love of mother for son, of father for daughter, the hatred of father by son, of mother by daughter – these are presented in such a way that they represent recognisable patterns in human behaviour. At times, O'Neill seems too clinical, as he was in *Strange Interlude*, especially when his characters blatantly analyse themselves and others. (Listen to Christine's words to Lavinia: 'You've tried to become the wife of your father and the mother of Orin! You've always schemed to steal my place!' Listen to Orin, staring at the dead Adam Brant: 'If I had been he I would have done what he did! I would have loved her as he loved her – and killed Father too – for her sake.')

But these moments do not diminish the force of the play's psychological determinism, which is rooted in the play's action and which reveals the truth of the characters' lives. The New England Puritanism, the Civil War, the chorus of townspeople, the 'escape' to the Blessed Isles, the pull of the sea (which one 'can't get near' because one is 'bound' to land and home – to use the words of 'Shenandoah', repeated throughout the trilogy) – these provide a natural and believable context to the characters' lives. The personal emotions that O'Neill gives to Ezra, Christine, Orin and Lavinia seem so natural to them, so true to their human nature, so true to the geography and history of their lives, that their characters are their destiny. Victims of their psyches, driven by their passions, haunted by the past that controls their present, they are as fated as the characters in Greek tragedy who are caught in the net of the gods. There is little difference between O'Neill and the Greeks in the force of the determinism which controls individual lives. The difference is in the nature of the determinism and its *effect*. Aeschylus ends his trilogy with Justice served and a new moral order established, justifying the ways of god to man. O'Neill ends with Lavinia entering a house of death to face her family's ghosts. Aeschylus's trilogy opens up; he faces the heavens in the bright light of an Athenian day. O'Neill's trilogy ends in a dark house behind a closed door and shuttered windows.

Lavinia's dark presence is felt throughout the play. Tall, thin, wearing black, her movements stiff, 'snapping out her words like an officer giving orders', she begins the play looking at her mother 'with an intense, bitter enmity'. The intensity of her hatred, the intensity of her passions throughout, including her love for the men in her life, gives her the kind of charisma tragedy demands of its heroines and heroes. Her emotions, true and deep, lead her down the darkening path of revenge and murder. She controls the play's action, just as she is controlled by her fate. She performs terrible deeds, and finally pays for these deeds, but she is also paying for being a Mannon, for being born to her condition – which makes her a victim as well as a victimiser. She has experienced happiness on the South Sea islands. As she tells Peter: 'I loved those Islands. They finished setting me free. There was something there mysterious and beautiful – a good spirit – of love – coming out of the land and sea. It made me forget death.' She recognises that life has other possibilities than living in the Mannon tomb, and she wishes to have that kind of life with Peter.

Oh, Peter, hold me close to you! I want to feel love. Love is all beautiful! I never used to know that! I was a fool! . . . We'll make an island for ourselves on land, and we'll have children and love them and teach them to love life so that they can never be possessed by hate and death!

But she immediately thinks of Orin, to whom she is tied by blood and guilt.

Soon thereafter Orin's incestuous approach to Lavinia leads to her 'horrified repulsion', which in turn leads to Orin's suicide. Orin goes to the peace of death, connected in his mind with the peace of the islands and the peace of Mother. For Lavinia, peace is too easy; she will face the dead, and we understand the difficulty of that choice precisely because she has had that *other* experience. She chooses hell over heaven. When she realises that her love for Adam Brant prodded her hatred for her mother, she says 'No' to the islands and to Peter. She realises that she deserves to be punished, and she makes herself the punisher. Acknowledging that she cannot escape the cage of family and self – asserting with finality, 'Always the dead between!' – facing the fact of fate, recognising the justice of her incarceration, she enters the house to *confront* the dead. Lavinia courageously walks into the Mannon tomb – she 'pivots sharply on her heel and marches woodenly into the house, closing the door behind her'.

At this moment, the tragic heroine Lavinia resembles most is Sophocles's Antigone, who also inherited her condition, who is filled with both love and hate, who travels a narrowing path to death, who enters her cave alone and resolute, despite the terror within. Lavinia's final act haunts the mind. It is the inevitable culmination of all the foreboding entrances to and exits from that awesome house. It is the ending O'Neill had in mind very early in the play's composition, according to his diary, and one feels that the whole play has been moving toward that ending. In a sense, the inevitability of the play's tragic progression is perfectly matched by the progression of scenes, meaning and form working together to lead to Lavinia's doom. O'Neill never gave any play of the twenties or thirties a better ending. Judging from the comments of reviewers, the ending provided a stunning theatrical moment for the first audiences. This praise by John Hutchens is not untypical:

In the moment when Lavinia, in black, stands framed between the white pillars of the House of Mannon, the sunset dying at her feet, the course of passion run – in that moment, playwright, performer and artist come together in a superb conclusion that belongs as completely and solely to the theatre as Mr O'Neill himself.[2]

Hutchens places the emphasis where it belongs, on O'Neill's sense of *theatre*. That O'Neill did not have the heightened language to give to his characters for this ambitious task of vying with the Greeks has been stated by many critics, and anticipated by O'Neill himself. 'It needed a great language to lift it beyond itself. I haven't got that.'[3] But his language – often more forceful and direct and moving than O'Neill realised – is combined with scenic devices (the setting, the use of light, the colour of costume, the repetitions of gesture and movement and song) to make *Mourning Becomes Electra*, despite its flaws, an impressive work of art. Not the least of its admirable qualities, often neglected in comparisons with Greek drama or in discussions of tragedy, is its ability to tell a story so well that an audience remains gripped for more than five hours, *interested* in the dramatised passions of a very small group of people. (Robert Benchley labelled the play 'good old-fashioned, spine-curling melo-drama', and said that O'Neill does 'thrill the bejeezes out of us!') [See Benchley's review in Section 2, above.] Planning carefully, using the resources of his theatre, O'Neill tells a big story about big passions, and he tells it with such truth that we get behind life and feel the real reality.

The play was given admirable direction by the Theatre Guild's Philip Moeller, a memorable set by Robert Edmond Jones, and superb acting by Alla Nazimova as Christine and Alice Brady as Lavinia. After the indulgences and excesses of the late twenties, O'Neill began the thirties with a realistic play that solidified his reputation as *the* American dramatist, and probably pushed him a giant step forward to the Nobel Prize for Literature in 1936. . . .

SOURCE: extract from ch. 6 ('The Thirties') in *Eugene O'Neill* – 'Macmillan Modern Dramatists' series (London & Basingstoke, 1982), pp. 106–18.

NOTES

1. The quotation is from O'Neill's 'Work Diary' – reproduced in section 1 of Part One, above.

2. John Hutchens's review, originally appearing in *Theatre Arts* (Jan. 1932), is reproduced in Oscar Cargill, N. Bryllion Fagin & William J. Fisher (eds), *O'Neill and His Plays* (New York, 1961), p. 193.

3. Quoted in Arthur Hobson Quinn, *A History of the American Drama* (New York, 1927), p. 258.

C. W. E. Bigsby   'Inner and Outer Worlds'   (1982)

. . . For O'Neill, the New England setting, redolent with notions of sin, guilt and punishment, and with Calvinist belief in determinism, was an entirely appropriate setting for such a trilogy. The self-destructive fatalism of Greek theatre, symbolised by the Furies, is transmuted into a Calvinist conscience which makes the self its own enemy. Love is corrupted by puritan values into lust, thus losing its redemptive and creative aspects. When Christine turns to Brant she is trying to restore a sense of romance and vitality to a world drained of life. For in the Mannon family values are so distorted that there is a psychic inbreeding, an anarchic inward-turned sexuality which is the mark and explanation of their self-destructiveness. The physical resemblance of the Mannons underlines this closed world which feeds off itself and breeds only death. The external world remains just that – external to their real concerns, barely intruding in the form of the local townspeople, who constitute a simple chorus, or the would-be lovers, Paul and Hazel, whose bland normality lacks the imaginative power to penetrate the psychological reflexiveness of the Mannons.

The mask-like faces, constantly referred to in the stage directions, are, as earlier in his work, an expression of his sense of the 'unreal behind what we call reality which is the real reality! – the unrealistic truth wearing the mask of lying reality' [O'Neill's 'Work Diary']. The psychology which is required to be the embodiment of this vision remains somewhat simplistic – the oedipal complex is here balanced by an electra complex (love of daughter for father) – setting up a dualism of false surface and true depth, a false mask and true face which rests rather too heavily on Freudian archetypes. But the mask is at least now generated by character. It is not only an image of a shared fate which links the Mannon family; it is also shaped by their own denial of change, of the living flux of experience, by an obsession with the past which allows the mask a dominance which denies the individual his individuality. In other words the notion of the mask becomes internal to the character, it becomes expressive of an interpretation of experience which concedes the authority to time, which allows no resistant self to violate the given. And this pattern of exterior and interior is reflected both in the stage set – the house itself being described as a mask – and in the formal structure of the play, which alternates exterior and interior scenes, scenes in which the external world impinges on, if it does not penetrate, the world of the Mannons, and those in which that world is absent.

The townsfolk who represent the external world are themselves seen only in their externals. Not merely are they a backdrop to the drama of the central characters – a chorus – but they are in some essential way characterless. They lack depth. If they suffer none of the extremes of the Mannon family, neither do they look into their own lives. At their most admirable they crystallise into the form of Peter and Hazel, the Starbucks of O'Neill's Melvillian drama; what he, in his notes, calls the 'untroubled, contented "good"', the sweet 'constant, unselfconscious, untempted virtue'. It is a telling description. We see no depth in the lives because there is none. They are not the material of tragedy.

And Melville is not an inappropriate name to invoke in a play in which *Typee* is quoted as an image of escape and release. The South Sea Island motif recurs as a symbol of a pre-lapsarian world, the world to which the principal characters are drawn. Here the rigid puritanism of New England would no longer apply. It is a place in which causality has no power, a pre-moral world. And yet, as in

Typee itself, there is a judgement to be made on a world so totally deprived of tension. For the price which the inhabitants of Melville's island pay for their paradise is the surrender of that intellectual perception which is the essence of individuation and the generating force of history. For a world deprived of pain, a world with no sense of sin, a world in which the pleasure principle dominates the reality principle, may also be a world without profundity, without energy; a world of surfaces, bland, homogeneous and ultimately static. Which is to say that the South Sea Island motif is also a part of the concern with masks, with levels of experience and perception which in some ways is the subject of the plays.

The sea is thus an escape which these characters cannot permit themselves or, rather, it is a world which they ultimately invest with their own fears and neuroses so that even this retreat is denied them. They are characters who, like Arthur Miller's, meet after the fall, and that fall is the source of their meaning. And although both male and female Mannons respond to the romantic spirit – Brant living for a time in the South Seas and Christine marrying Ezra for his romantic quality – that aspect of their character is always held in check by the gravitational pull of their Calvinist consciences, or their inability to break free of their heritage, to challenge the happiness which seems too insubstantial to their spirits. Vengeance, for them, is a way of challenging the world as it is. They wish to recreate it, to mould it in such a way that it will meet the demands of their insistent consciences. They are creator-destroyers whose dignity lies in their acceptance of total responsibility for their actions. David, Christine and Orin Mannon even assume the godlike attribute in taking their own lives, as the latter two and Brant had taken those of others. If social propriety, morality and religion stand between them and their objectives then they will ignore them as Ahab was willing to challenge the sun itself. This is their folly and their greatness. And if both Lavinia and Orin are tempted to lay aside their severe view of the world, to settle for the romantic mask, this is a temptation which their own inherited nature will not finally allow. The world of innocence is, after all, not recoverable.

What O'Neill calls the 'simple sad rhythm of hopeless sea longing', represented by the reiterated singing of the sea shanty, 'Shenandoah', is rejected in favour of a relentless engagement with the self. Indeed, this is a world in which the only authority is self. The many crimes of the play go unpunished. In fact, for all the blandness of the immediate vicinity, the world which they inhabit is itself in a state of collapse. Orin returns from a war in which words like 'dignity' and 'glory' and 'honour' have been as effectively eroded as Frederic

Henry had felt them to be in *A Farewell to Arms*. America, too, is a house which has been at war with itself, like the Mannons. And Lincoln's death denies even the apparent restoration of order. It is not simply a case of the Mannons inhabiting their own antinomian world; the whole world envisaged by the play is deprived of order, form and meaning.

And yet O'Neill still wishes to set them apart. Hence his dramatic isolation of the house from the town and his notion of the characters as locked up behind their own deterministic masks. They are the forces of death and their faces are like death masks. The impetus is towards destruction and death. The only force which holds them back is love and O'Neill sets up a Freudian battle between the ego, or death instinct, and the id, or life instinct, with his thumb securely on one side of the scale. The death-mask make-up becomes an expression of that inanimate state which can only be vivified by passion – a passion which at times disrupts the mask but which eventually becomes the agent of the death instinct in a world as completely inverted as that which the Mannons inhabit. Indeed Ezra Mannon, a death dealer both as a judge and a soldier, is given the speech, quoted above, which is a simple paraphrase of Freud's observation in *Beyond the Pleasure Principle*: 'Life was a dying. Being born was starting to die. Death was being born.'

And so O'Neill establishes a *mise-en-scène* which reflects his dramatic strategy in the play. We move from an external to an internal view of the world which he creates and the characters who inhabit it. The audience is confronted with a special curtain which shows the house as it is seen from the street. From this, as he explained in a descriptive note, 'in each play one comes to the exterior of the house in the opening act and enters it in the following act'.

But, despite O'Neill's suggestion of a gap separating the Mannons from their society, it is clear that in this regard at least they are scarcely aberrant. The iconographic significance of the town's white church is as usurped by irony as that of the similarly white Mannon house. If the Mannons splatter that whiteness with blood then so too does the world beyond their estate. As Ezra himself replies, when charged by his wife with being obsessed with death (an ironic charge of course since she is at that moment plotting his murder):

How in hell people ever got such notions! That white meeting-house. It stuck in my mind – clean-scrubbed and white-washed – a temple of death. But in this war I've seen too many white walls splattered with blood that counted no more than dirty water. I've seen dead men scattered about, no more important than rubbish to be got rid of. That made the white meeting-house seem meaningless – making so much solemn fuss over death!

It is not only the Mannons who are death-centred; it is the world which they inhabit.

If the mask stood as a barrier between the Mannons and life, it also stood as a barrier between themselves and other people. In particular Ezra belatedly realises that there has been a barrier between himself and his wife, a gulf which he tries first to bridge with words and then with passion. But they are shut up inside themselves, so in love with their own conception of themselves that only a mirror image of that self can make a suitable mate. And so Orin loves his mother, and his sister when she takes on the appearance of that mother. By the same token Lavinia loves her father, and the image of that father which she detects in Brant. And so the circle closes, a series of repetitive actions reflected in the reiterative structure of the play, the echoic nature of some of the lines, and the fundamental strategy of creating characters who are themselves the mirror images of their own parents. The principal force of the play lies in O'Neill's dramatisation of this desire to embrace one's own image – an egotism which can only be death-oriented. The play ends as Lavinia's bid to escape her fate founders when, with a literally Freudian slip, she addresses Peter, the man who could release her, by the name of her mother's lover. This reflexive truth traps her and she retreats into the house, earlier described as a tomb, the last Mannon. Ibsen signifies the freedom of Nora with the sound of the door slamming as she leaves the house which has become the image of her mental and moral subservience. O'Neill ends his trilogy with the sound of the shutters slamming shut as Lavinia enters the house, closing the door behind her. With this action she wilfully retreats into the inner world which the house has symbolised.

Mourning Becomes Electra is an advance in that he has learned to subordinate theatrical devices to psychological needs. As he wrote in a letter to Kenneth Macgowan in 1929, 'No more sets or theatrical devices as anything but unimportant background – except in the most imperatively exceptional case where organically they belong.' His imagination was now more firmly under control and the energy was not dissipated by diverting it into a self-conscious concern with mechanism. Here, everything was to be seen through, or to serve, character. . . .

Viewed in one way the fallibility of the Mannons derives from their tendency to see the world in simple terms: passion must be pursued, slights must be avenged, problems must be resolved by violent action. And yet this process is compounded by a dramatist who applies a similar Manichaean model to the world which he creates. The psychology is imposed on the character rather than derived from it as it would be in *Long Day's Journey Into Night* (1956). Both myth and psychological model are too close to the surface. What we see is character as exemplification and action as reenactment of archetype. George Steiner rightly objects, in *The Death of Tragedy* [1961], to 'the lesser men' (O'Neill, Giraudoux, Hofmannsthal, Cocteau) who 'often proceed with wanton artifice' trying to 'have it both ways, combining the resonance of the classic theme with the savour of the new'. He complains that such writers set ambushes for the imagination, setting off majestic echoes through reliance on familiar stories. O'Neill, in particular, attracts his opprobrium because he 'commits inner vandalism by sheer inadequacy of style. In the morass of his language,' Steiner asserts, 'the high griefs of the house of Atreus dwindle to a case of adultery and murder in some provincial rathole.' The objection may be unnecessarily patrician, and his notion that 'half the work is done for the poet before the curtain rises' a failure to recognise the special problems of transforming classical models, but he is right in identifying O'Neill's failure to produce an adequate modern equivalent for a classic resonance, and right, too, in identifying his stylistic and linguistic inadequacies. The speech of the Mannons is deliberately contrasted with that of the townspeople. The latter speak in banalities, a flatness of perception underlined by the use of dialect. The Mannons converse at a high emotional intensity, with neurotic directness. All tensions, pains and fears are allowed to bubble to the surface in language, discharging themselves in words. The effect is an hysterical intensity which permits little variation beyond the simple contrast between the Mannons and the others. The emotional and linguistic range of the Mannons is severely restricted and this underscores the melodramatic nature of the action. The inner life tends to rush into an outer existence in a way which is neither psychologically nor poetically convincing. The tension between inner and outer world is lost. Everything must be stated just as every whim must be pursued to the point of action. And the result is a kind of banality which is not restricted to a linguistic sphere. And if, in a sense, it is the fate of the Mannons to be fully known, that explicitness is the undoing of the plays as well as of the characters. Language loses the tension which comes from the unspoken, from that which is concealed from the speaker as well as from the listener. And that tension, that energy, is replaced, in the text, by the exclamation mark, a sign which signifies a truth flourished openly and therefore a truth which has lost much of its kinetic energy. Indeed, the very supposed rationality of the psychological analysis on which the play rests neutralises the tragic impulse. The inscrutable forces behind life which he had set himself to expose at the beginning of his career have become all too scrutable. Psychopathology is finally no substitute for the tragic imagination.

Mourning Becomes Electra did, however, indicate a direction in O'Neill's work which was to lead eventually to the achievement of his final plays. The landscape which he describes here is a landscape of the mind. And in moving through the gauze curtain, which his stage directions indicated should be painted with the social location of the Mannon estate, through the external walls of the house to the interior, we are moving from the social to the psychological, from the public to the private – a path which took O'Neill to his central subject, a Strindbergian drama of sexual tension and moral implosion. As he had said earlier in his career, '[man's] struggle used to be with the gods, but is now with himself, his own past'. . . .

SOURCE: extract from chapter on O'Neill in *Twentieth-Century American Drama*: I, *1900–1940* (Cambridge, 1982), pp. 80–4, 86–7.

Egil Tornqvist   'Green Paganism and Gray Puritanism'   (1969)

. . . *Desire Under the Elms* ends with the Sheriff's envious remark: 'It's a jim-dandy farm, no denyin'. Wished I owned it!' The line is starkly ironical. The curse of the land, of material possessions, has just been forcefully brought home to us. Then comes the ignorant outsider and declares that he wishes to possess that which has brought only misery to its possessors. The Sheriff and his companions are comparable to the town choruses in *Electra*, which also see without seeing and lack the moral stature of the main characters. His words could have been ours, had we not witnessed the Cabot tragedy. They express precisely what we feel at the beginning of *Mourning Becomes Electra*, when we take in the '*special curtain*', showing the extensive Mannon estate. This curtain may in a sense be regarded as a fragmentary counterpart of the widely known myth the Greek tragedians could rely on. For it offers the audience a background story of sorts and introduces it to the major conflict in the trilogy, that between green 'paganism' and gray puritanism. What we see is the Mannon house surrounded by rich vegetation.

'*As seen from the street*', i.e. from the perspective of the town-dwellers (the world outside including the audience), the estate with its '*extensive grounds*' is most impressive. Significantly there is nothing in O'Neill's description of the house as depicted on the curtain that makes us think otherwise. From a distance it appears 'purty' to us as it does to the town chorus. We too are under the illusion that what we see is, to use the Sheriff's words in *Desire*, 'a jim-dandy farm'. Thus, even before the play has begun, we are grouped with the chorus, 'the world outside which always sees without really seeing or understanding' (O'Neill, 1931).

Once inside the estate we can better see what the house is like; the stage directions for Act One read in part:

At front is the driveway which leads up to the house from the two entrances on the street. Behind the driveway the white Grecian temple portico with its six tall columns extends across the stage. A big pine tree is on the lawn at the edge of the drive before the right corner of the house. Its trunk is a black column in striking contrast to the white columns of the portico. . . .

It is shortly before sunset and the soft light of the declining sun shines directly on the front of the house, shimmering in a luminous mist on the white portico and the gray stone wall behind, intensifying the whiteness of the columns, the somber grayness of the wall, the green of the open shutters, the green of the lawn and shrubbery, the black and green of the pine tree. The white columns cast black bars of shadow on the gray wall behind them. The windows of the lower floor reflect the sun's rays in a resentful glare. The temple portico is like an incongruous white mask fixed on the house to hide its somber gray ugliness.

Surrounded by 'the green beauty of their land', the Mannons – so the curtain told us – 'live in as near the Garden of Paradise . . . as you'll find on this earth', to quote Brant's description of the South Sea islands. Or so they would if it was not for the house. After generations of nature-trimming puritanism Abe Mannon, out of revenge on the love he was incapable of himself and which was therefore denied him by Marie Brantôme, tore down the old mansion and built his monstrous 'temple of Hate and Death'. Yet the vegetation that still surrounds the Mannon estate indicates that nature and the spirit of love, if repressed, are not extinguished. The white portico, like the puritan version of the story, which is the one offered to the world, is a false façade hiding the grim truth visualised in the house itself, the truth, which says that hatred rather than righteousness and revenge rather than justice, motivated Abe's destruction of the old house and erection of the present one.

Visualising modern man's dilemma, the Mannon house is fittingly a 'grotesque perversion of everything Greek temple expressed of meaning of life' (O'Neill, 1931). In its imitation of pagan love of life, beauty and purity, the portico is incongruously a part of the puritan house built in hatred of life and love; it is itself a perversion of the pagan spirit, for its whiteness is biblical and sepulchral rather than Greek.

The inescapability of the fate is underlined by the static setting: the house – exterior or interior – is nearly always before our eyes. Only once – in the ship scene close to the middle of the trilogy (Part II, Four) – do the Mannons get away from it. Here, for a brief moment, the sea promises 'escape and release' (O'Neill, 1931), but the escape is illusory and the main effect of this futile attempt at breakthrough is, in fact, a strengthening of the feeling that the characters are chained to the house, doomed to spend their lives in it. Fittingly, Ezra, Christine, Orin and eventually, we must assume, Lavinia all die in the house which symbolises the Mannon way of life, in the house which has worked their destruction: Ezra in the matrimonial bed which he had abused by his inability to love his wife naturally; Christine in the room where she succumbed to the evil Mannon spirit the moment she decided to murder her husband; Orin in the room where his mother committed suicide, partly due to his Mannon harshness.

The house is like a monster swallowing its own breed. Its windows are *'revengeful eyes'*, rejecting rather than accepting the warm sunlight, and the shutters are like eyelids. The play begins with open windows and shutters, but when Ezra returns the windows and shutters are closed; the house front becomes a death mask, expressive both of Ezra's life-denying puritanism and Christine's evil spirit. When Ezra tells her about the Mannon death worship, she keeps her eyes closed, her face resembling a death mask, indicating that she is a victim of the very tradition he is commenting on and which is expressed in the house front. He asks her to open her eyes, but almost immediately entreats her to close them again – an illustration, it seems, of Ezra's willingness but utter inability to free Christine of her death mask. The shutters remain closed also after Ezra's death, for with his corpse in it, the house is literally a tomb, and besides it is now Lavinia who rules the house.

In the third part Lavinia's attitude has changed. It is now Orin who locks himself up behind closed blinds in the study, hiding from the world with his guilt. Lavinia, on the other hand, is firmly determined to drive the ghosts away. She has strength enough to open the shutters in the study, claiming that the air in it is 'suffocating' for Orin – as indeed it will shortly prove to be: soon he is to kill himself in the study. It is also due to her that the shutters are fastened back and that the windows are open in the final act. With Orin dead and escape from the Mannons imminent, Lavinia repeats her mother's worship of light and air. Then, in a crushing *anagnorisis*, she discovers that she can rid herself of the evil Mannon spirit only by living with it. She closes her eyes, that is, she 'dies'. And, '*without opening her eyes*', she says, '*strangely, as if to herself*: "Why can't the dead die!"'. She is not merely thinking of the Mannon ghosts; she is also addressing herself, wishing her own death. 'Dead' herself now, it only remains for her, the last Mannon, to prepare her own tomb. She orders the shutters nailed tight and buries herself in the darkened house.

Of the rich vegetation revealed in the special curtain, the stage picture shows only the blooming lilac shrubbery on the left and one of the pine trees on the right. Christine is linked with the shrubbery; she appears close to it twice on her way to and back from the flower garden, the second time carrying a bunch of flowers. The pine tree is visually linked with the house, the dark green of its needles matching the '*dark green*' shutters, its column-like trunk in form resembling the house columns and in colour the '*black bars*' they cast on the house, turning it, as it were, into a prison. As an evergreen never visibly in bloom (and in this respect contrasting with the rest of the surrounding vegetation) and mournful in color, it adequately expresses the Mannon sterility and hatefulness.

When O'Neill at one point makes Ezra appear close to and turned towards the pine tree, he may wish to underline the fact that the man's feelings of hatred and jealousy do not merely concern the present situation but also a traumatic experience in the past. Christine's rejection of him (in favor of Brant) reminds him of Marie Brantôme who similarly 'rejected' him and his father Abe, in favor of David.

More obviously, Lavinia is connected with the pine tree, her black costume in color resembling the trunk of the tree. We are reminded of that especially towards the very end when Lavinia, like '*an ebony pillar*' – O'Neill's description of the pine tree – '*woodenly*' passes between the white columns of the house on her way into its gloomy darkness. Six unnatural deaths – those of David, Marie, Ezra, Adam, Christine and Orin – have occurred in the family since Abe Mannon built his 'temple of Hate and Death'; there are six puritan columns in front of the tomblike house. Differing from the other Mannons – except Abe – both by her excessive guilt and by her decision to punish herself to death-in-life, Lavinia is like a seventh black column matching the tree, symbol of the Mannons', especially Abe's, life hatred. As hateful as the grandfather, she has no Mannon to punish – but herself.

Unlike the pine trees, the rest of the vegetation is light green – it is either spring or summer – and subordinated to the seasonal and life-like rhythm of budding, blooming, decay, death. As we have noted, it links the estate with the islands. This is especially true of the flowers, worn by the natives in Dionysian fashion, 'stuck over their ears', symbols of youthful innocence, happiness and love. Thus Christine's brightening up of the Mannon 'tomb' with flowers is not merely a sign of her joyous acceptance of Brant, her lover, or even of her attempt to transform the deadly house into a temple of love. As an unhappy, ageing and guilt-ridden woman – she is already planning to murder her husband – Christine longs for all the values represented by the flowers. Her act is one of exorcism.

This is even more true of Lavinia in the final act. Repeating her mother's flower-picking, she is much more desperate. Filling every room in the house with flowers, she frankly tells Peter: 'Take me in this house of the dead and love me! Our love will drive the dead away!' But her black costume, unlike her mother's green, harmonises, not with the flowers, but with the dark pine tree. At last she realises and accepts her Mannon nature. Her final words are: '. . . tell Hannah to throw out all the flowers'. Innocence, happiness and love are incompatible with the Mannon house and do not become Lavinia. It adds considerably to her tragic stature that, despite the intense love for flowers she has just demonstrated, she has the strength to condemn herself to a life without them. . . .

SOURCE: extract from *A Drama of Souls: Studies in O'Neill's Super-Naturalistic Techniques* (New Haven, Conn., 1969), pp. 62–6.

Robert B. Heilman   'Melodrama of Disaster'
(1973)

. . . *Mourning Becomes Electra* (1931), which translates into modern American idiom Agamemnon's return from Troy and the succeeding events in his family (the Mannons at their New England Mycenae after the Civil War), takes in much less territory than *Strange Interlude* (1928). The greater compression helps invigorate and intensify an

ingenious, though sometimes laborious, transposition of myth into
modern terms of motivation and sensibility. Into the speech, flat
and prosy as it tends to be, O'Neill has got a pressure and vehemence
that make for authenticity. In modernising, O'Neill makes some key
omissions, and what he does not see (and for that matter, what he
sees) in the Mycenaean myth is a key to his way of dealing with
tragic materials. For instance, he omits the Cassandra figure and
the solid strength of the returning conqueror; Ezra shrinks into a
minor commander who is almost pathetically trying to break the
wall between Christine and himself, and who seems a sad little
victim. In motivating Christine's animus against her husband,
O'Neill uses two devices that work against grandeur of effect. He
omits the sacrifice of Iphigenia and substitutes a 'sacrifice' of Orin:
General Mannon had made him go to war, where Orin had suffered
almost fatal head wounds. Hence Christine's maternal resentment
serves mainly to illustrate the mother-son affinity (an old O'Neill
theme), which is pushed very hard in scene after scene. Even before
this, we find, Christine had been disgusted by Ezra on their wedding
night and had never forgiven him. Not only does this history render
her romantic passion for Brant questionable, but it is a come-down
from the queenly vindictiveness of Clytemnestra.

O'Neill tends to constrict the legend by naturalising it in clinical
terms, especially of types of sexual conduct that, however universal,
have here got out of hand and disturbed the personalities. He
employs mother-son, father-daughter, and brother-sister patterns of
incestuous feeling, and introduces incest implicitly into Christine's
liaison by making Captain Brant (the Aegisthus figure) a first cousin
of Ezra Mannon. Orin's head wound gives him a psychic shakiness
which, added to his oedipality, means that under stress he will not
find purgation through misery but will simply get sicker and sicker.
This world closes in upon itself; instead of convincing us of its
representativeness, it keeps circumscribing its relevance.

Ironically, this movement away from largeness takes place in
characters who are tragic in conception. They are virtually all
divided characters. Their divisions are of the peculiarly modern sort;
they feel the pressure of clashing impulses, hardly at all that of
imperatives. Lavinia keeps talking about her 'duty' to her father,
but we are to see this as a rationalisation of her strong, if
unrecognised, sexual feeling for him. Whereas Orestes felt both the
obligation to avenge the murder of his father, and the counter-
obligation of filial piety, Orin's motive is jealousy of his mother's
lover; and Lavinia's interest in the death of Brant, though less visible
because of her own self-deception, is of the same kind (Brant had

intensified Lavinia's hatred of her mother by loving her mother instead of her). Yet if the motivations are mechanical, the Mannon actions take on a moral complexion by becoming unsatisfactory to the agents; quite aside from the agonizing quest for security (the Macbeth vein), the Mannons crave something more durable than the catharsis of destructive jealousy and hate. They have a sense of impending judgement. Their feeling of guilt goes hand-in-hand with a dream of 'love' and 'life' elsewhere, outside; each has the possibility, or the hope, of a saving relationship with another – Christine with Brant, Orin with Hazel Niles, and Lavinia with Peter Niles (when they are on stage, the Nileses create a sense of a well world utterly different from that of the Mannons). But though the Mannons yearn for salvation through the love of these others, they are even more strongly driven by the family heritage, with its mixture of perverse love and vindictive hate, of jealousy and of tensions that break out into violence, its severity and wilfulness that sometimes appear as 'duty', its sense of immitigable punishment, of threatening and inescapable ghosts. (The talk of 'the past,' 'the house', and 'the dead' is remarkably like that in Ibsen's *Rosmersholm*.) They cannot find tragic purgation; they turn inward and downward.

O'Neill's treatment of guilt reveals his antitragic perspective. For the Mannons, guilt is only a chain, or, as Orin puts it, the 'darkness of death in life' [Part III, Act Two]. Yet the ability to know and to feel guilt is a mark of tragic sentience; without it, a character is villain or moral vegetable, too limited to be intrinsically interesting. Furthermore, it is a possible avenue to well-being; it is that coming to consciousness of one's history through which one may enter into a new history. It is that acknowledgement of the past that holds out some assurance of a future. Orin contributes to the suicide of his mother by killing her lover Brant, then is divided in what he wants to do after murder. On the one hand he can tell Lavinia that their only way to salvation is to 'Confess and atone to the full extent of the law!' [III, Two], and he can write a family history as a part of 'man's feeble striving to understand himself' [III, Three]; on the other hand he wants to use this history to keep Lavinia from marrying Peter Niles and then to bind her to himself through the guilt of incest. Though he longs to 'confess to [Hazel's] purity' and 'be forgiven' [III, Two], the obsessive involvement with his sister prevents his putting his longing into effect, and he commits suicide. Lavinia is equally split. She complains bitterly of Orin's 'stupid guilty conscience' but adds, like Rebecca West to Rosmer, 'You're becoming my guilty conscience, too!' [III, Two]. On the other hand, 'There is nothing to confess! There was only justice! . . . You're too

vile to live! You'd kill yourself if you weren't a coward' [III, Three].
And again, 'I'm not asking God or anybody for forgiveness. I forgive
myself!' [III, Four]. At the end, however, after she has driven her
lover away and turned to the house: 'I've got to punish myself!
Living alone here with the dead is a worse act of justice than death
or prison! I'll never go out or see anyone! ... I'll live alone with
the dead ...' [III, Four]. While Orin has chosen death, Lavinia has
shut herself up in a living death. The tragic division has found a
solution only in illness; the normal contradictoriness of life has led
to a clinical flight from life – into the grave and the hospital. The
vindictive need to punish others has metamorphosed into the need
to punish oneself, the soul on the road to light has become
irretrievably fixed in the darkness of self-flagellation. (Thirty-five
years before, Hardy pictured this outcome in Sue Bridehead; twenty
years after O'Neill, Duerrenmatt saw it in Mr Mississippi.) Illness
is not tragic; what we have here is again a drama of disaster, the
disaster of personality, with all the intensity that the narrower form
can generate.

The world of the play keeps closing in, as we have said, cutting
itself off from the full human cosmos. This is symbolised not only in
the last and best remembered action of the play – Lavinia's shutting
herself in the house for good – but in the incestuous longings that
cut off the outer life where salvation might lie. Here, in this drawing
back into sickness, death and death-in-life, is O'Neill's sharpest
departure from Aeschylus. What O'Neill did not comprehend in
Aeschylus, or chose to reject, was the *Eumenides*, that imaginatively
structured third drama in which Aeschylus made every effort to
'open out' the myth, to bring it into the widest stream of significance,
to catch all its reverberations for humanity at large. Orestes is
caught, not in an infantile emotion, but in a terrible conflict that
has to be debated on the Areopagus, and evokes strife among the
gods; the closeness of the vote attests to the almost equal strength
of the claims upon a humanity gifted with the sentience to respond
to them. Though he never imagines that he can act without suffering,
which indeed becomes illness, Orestes is unwilling to accept his
immense act of penance as everlasting, but struggles, literally and
symbolically, to turn from the agonised payment of a debt and
return to ordinary life. Finally, Athena's persuading the Erinyes to
accept their new role as Eumenides is an extraordinary symbolic
drama, for through it, as Maud Bodkin has shown,[1] we understand
the conversion of primitive energy, without its simply becoming
innocuous, from a destructive to a beneficent function. This may be
considered a turning point in the history of human potentiality.

It is just this turning point that O'Neill does not reach. *Mourning Becomes Electra* stays in that narrow, stern, unalterable region in which, once man comes under the hand of the Erinyes, he is always under the hand of the Erinyes. He falls into the egotism of permanent disaster. As Orin sums up, 'The only love I can know now is the love of guilt for guilt which breeds more guilt – until you get so deep at the bottom of hell there is no lower you can sink and you rest there in peace!' [III, Three]. It carries on, to a more desperate misery, the quest for punishment of *Strange Interlude* (1928), the pathetic vital inadequacy of men in *Beyond the Horizon* (1920) and *The Great God Brown* (1926), the oppressive closing-in that afflicts the protagonists of *The Emperor Jones* (1920) and *All God's Chillun* (1924); it anticipates the pitiable in-turning wretchedness of *Long Day's Journey* (1956) and *A Moon for the Misbegotten* (1952). But the perspective of *Mourning Becomes Electra* is most interesting in its kinship with that of *The Iceman Cometh* (1946), which O'Neill would write within a decade. The two plays are complementary in the anti-tragic bias. In *Iceman* O'Neill implicitly argued the impossibility of tragic experience: man cannot bear self-knowledge. He must therefore live in illusion, protected by a cordon sanitaire from the monstrous infection of truth. For once that infection has reached him – as in *Mourning Becomes Electra* – it will be so terrible that it will kill him or make him a lifelong invalid. In O'Neill's hopeless view, man has only two choices with regard to the evil blight of self-knowledge – total immunity or total contamination, ignorance or ruin.

Iceman deals with derelicts, *Mourning* with aristocracy. *Iceman* . . . has some remarkable similarities to [Gorky's] *The Lower Depths*. *Mourning* is the lower depths of the upper crust, the Inferno of those privileged to know something of what they are, but sharing with all degrees that corruption of the will that tyrannises over O'Neill's field of vision. It is Christine Mannon who says, 'Now I know there is only hell!' [II, Five]. The play as a whole supports her: there is only an Inferno, no Purgatorio. This is the dark record of total catastrophe, not the tragic account of experience. But as melodrama of disaster, it has the massiveness of total conviction. . . .

SOURCE: extract from *The Iceman, The Arsonist and The Troubled Agent* (Seattle, 1973), pp. 99–104.

NOTE

1. Notably in *Archetypal Patterns in Poetry: Psychological Studies of Imagination* (Oxford, 1934) and *Studies of Type-Images in Poetry, Religion and Philosophy* (Oxford, 1951).

Raymond Williams   Private Tragedy   (1966)

. . . More clearly than Strindberg, O'Neill identified the family as a destructive entity, especially in *Mourning Becomes Electra* and *Long Day's Journey Into Night*. A speech in *The Great God Brown* (1926) is characteristic, when a son mourns his father:

What aliens we were to each other! When he lay dead, his face looked so familiar that I wondered where I had met that man before. Only at the second of my conception. After that, we grew hostile with concealed shame.

The emphasis, here, is not only on the inherent hostility and guilt, but also on the fact of recognition in death, when, paradoxically, some kind of living contact can at last be made. The primary relationships are in experience a profound alienation, and the self that emerged from them is a ghost who will struggle to touch life at some point, but who in the pain of this knows unreality as the greater reality. These are the 'fog people' of *Long Day's Journey Into Night*. Edmund, describing being out in the fog, says:

Everything looked and sounded unreal. That's what I wanted – to be alone with myself in another world where truth is untrue and life can hide from itself. . . . The fog and the sea seemed part of each other. It was like walking on the bottom of the sea. As if I had drowned long ago. As if I was a ghost belonging to the fog, and the fog was the ghost of the sea. It felt damned peaceful to be nothing more than a ghost within a ghost.

And later:

It was a great mistake, my being born a man, I would have been much more successful as a sea-gull or a fish. As it is, I will always be a stranger who never feels at home, who does not really want and is not really wanted, who can never belong, who must always be a little in love with death.

Long Day's Journey Into Night is O'Neill's version of himself and his own family, and it is easy to hear the intensity of this feeling. The pattern of particular relationships, and of the individuals composing them, can be seen as leading, perhaps even inevitably, to this kind of consciousness. Yet what we overlook, in such arguments for authenticity, is that the pattern itself is a creation of this conscious-ness, and a kind of justification for it. This is the point about a self-reflecting empiricism, made earlier. It is not, in the end, that the relationships create the consciousness. Dramatically, it is the consciousness that creates the relationships. What looks like a family drama is an isolate drama.

The point comes out most clearly in *Mourning Becomes Electra*. O'Neill said that he was trying here

to get modern psychological approximation of the Greek sense of fate into such a play, which an intelligent audience of today, possessed of no beliefs in gods or supernatural retribution, could accept and be moved by.

The statement has a representative importance, including the reference to modern psychology. What is being offered is not primarily a set of destructive relationships, but a pattern of fate which is not dependent on any beliefs outside man. Life itself is fate, in this fundamental pattern, which is again the inherently self-destructive family. The critical difficulty, always, is that the fatal pattern is then given particularity; it is even possible to consider and confirm it along quite different lines: New England puritanism, the effects of civil war, and so on. But this, both critically and dramatically, is a false particularity. What matters, clearly, is the imposed pattern, which has the effect of conferring a sense of inevitability on what, as experience, was and could otherwise be seen as a series of living choices. The pattern comes from the consciousness of the isolate, rationalised by reference to modern psychology and to the Greeks. In this relatively constant progress from possibility to inevitability, and from the authentically particular to the willed general, it is important to distinguish a play like *Mourning Becomes Electra*, with its external elements of generalisation in the Greek analogy, from a play like *Long Day's Journey Into Night*, where the generalisation is more truly internal, and to that extent more moving.

In his reworking of the *Oresteia*, O'Neill substituted psychology for the Greek action. What is less often noticed is that this psychology is curiously static: underlying and determinist, rather than active and living. In the end it is not so much that the relationships are destructive as that they are illusory:

MANNON: . . . Me as your husband being killed, that seemed queer and wrong – like something dying that had never lived.

From this basic reality of relationship, the patterns of adultery and incest follow as it were mechanically. The pain and misdirection are bred in the original nullity. The only active feeling is the struggle of these ghosts to come alive, of these dead to awaken. Nothing is possible within this house and this family; the dream of the happy islands is of a totally alternative condition. Yet for all the careful grafting of the Freudian pattern, this is not psychology, but metaphysics: the characteristic metaphysics of the isolate, for whom life in any form but the suffering of frustration and loss is impossible. The characteristic resolution is neither Greek nor Freudian, but simply the achievement of death, which because there is no God has to be self-inflicted, by suicide or total withdrawal:

LAVINIA: I'm the last Mannon. I've got to punish myself. Living alone here with the dead is a worse act of justice than death or prison. I'll never go out or see anyone. I'll have the shutters nailed close so no sunlight can ever get in. I'll live alone with the dead, and keep their secrets and let them hound me, until the curse is paid out and the last Mannon is let die. [*With a strange cruel smile of gloating over the years of self-torture*] I know they will see to it I live for a long time! It takes the Mannons to punish themselves for being born.

The analogy of Mannon seems finally not to Agamemnon but to Man. . . .

SOURCE: extract from chapter ('Private Tragedy') in *Modern Tragedy* (London, 1966; Stanford, Calif., 1966), pp. 116–19.

St John Ervine   'He Dares Comparison with Aeschylus'   (1948)

[This criticism of *Mourning Becomes Electra* is part of Ervine's general attack on O'Neill, centred round the *TLS* essay dealing mainly with *The Iceman Cometh*, included in section 3 of Part Two, below – Ed.]

. . . Mr O'Neill's supreme challenge to the classics was made in *Mourning Becomes Electra*, where he dares comparison with Aeschylus in the *Oresteia*. He is, of course, as much entitled to take the Aeschylean theme and set it in the period of the Civil War as Shakespeare was to rewrite Hamlet; but when a man borrows on that scale, he should be careful to surpass or, at least, be equal with the lender. It is a mistake to think you are Shakespeare when you are manifestly Kyd. *Mourning Becomes Electra* is Mr O'Neill's masterpiece, and is superbly constructed. In no other work, except the charming, almost conventional, comedy, *Ah, Wilderness!* – a surprising piece, because of its sanity and normal, likable people – does Mr O'Neill display so much virtuosity. But we have a different tale to tell when we come to the spiritual values of the trilogy.

Clytemnestra had several reasons for murdering Agamemnon, apart from any over-ruling power which may have compelled her to commit the crime, and the most potent of them was the sacrifice of Iphigenia. But what compulsion had Christine Mannon to murder her husband? The house possessed of an evil is an element in the two trilogies, but a religious belief supports that of Aeschylus. What supports Mr O'Neill's Christine makes a vague complaint against Mannon's behaviour on her wedding night.[1] Her romance, for she had loved the handsome soldier, had turned that night to disgust. Yet she had lived with him for a quarter of a century! . . . Clytemnestra never loved Agamemnon. She was, like Cassandra, one of his spoils of war. 'By force you wedded me', she cries in *Iphigenia in Aulis* [by Euripedes – Ed.].

> I never loved you. Tantalus you slew,
> My first dear husband; and my little son
> You tore from my breast.

Nevertheless she had been a good and submissive wife to Agamemnon, bearing him three daughters and a son, and would have remained so had he not committed the final, unforgivable crime against her. Himself a superstitious man, he had sought to put heart in his sullen soldiers by sacrificing their eldest daughter at the suggestion of Calchas the priest. And for what?

> To win back Helen. Your own child for a wanton,
> Your dearest for a foe!

Euripedes puts bitter words on Clytemnestra's lips, but who will deny that they were justified? Is there any motive in Christine Mannon's mind equal to hers? Christine is not a spoil of war, the widow of a slain soldier, the mother of a son murdered by the man she must now marry. Nor has her daughter by this Agamemnon been sacrificed in appeasement of frivolous and whimsical gods in a war for a premature film star. Compared with Clytemnestra, Christine is motiveless: a mawkish schoolgirl with a crude, novelettish mind. Psychoanalysis, as it is understood in Greenwich Village, plays havoc with Mr O'Neill's thought in this play, as it does in a badly bungled piece, *Strange Interlude*, where ideas on neurology are as far removed from fact as Ibsen's idea of inherited taint in *Ghosts*. Artists who meddle with raw science and rawer medicine are apt to ruin themselves. . . .

SOURCE: extract from article ('Counsels of Despair') in the *Times Literary*

Supplement (10 April 1948) – authorship anonymous, as the journal's convention was until the late 1970s.

NOTE

1. [Ed.] 'What supports . . . wedding night.' – Ervine's intended meaning is evidently garbled here.

Eric Bentley   'Cultural and Psychological Gas'   (1952)

. . . the more he attempts, the less he achieves. *Lazarus Laughed* and *The Great God Brown* and *Days Without End* are inferior to *The Emperor Jones* and *Anna Christie* and *Ah, Wilderness!* O'Neill has never learned his lesson. The idea of 'big work' lured him out into territory where his sensibility is entirely inoperative. Even his most ardent admirers have little to say in favor of *Dynamo*, the only play where he frontally assails the problem of 'the death of an old God and the failure of science'. A hundred novelists have dealt more subtly with hidden motives than O'Neill did in his famous essay in psychological subtlety, *Strange Interlude*, a play that is equally inferior as a study of upper-class Americans. Then there is his desire to re-create ancient tragedy. Although no one is more conscious than he that America is not an Athens, the 'Greek dream' – the desire to be an Aeschylus – has been his nightmare.

The classic and notorious problem about tragedy in modern dress has been that the characters, not being over life-size but rather below it, excite pity without admiration and therefore without terror. Though O'Neill has talked of an 'ennobling identification' with protagonists, he has only once tried to do anything about it: only in *Mourning Becomes Electra* are the characters over life-size. Unhappily this is not because of the size of their bones but, as it were, by inflation with gas, cultural and psychological.

The cultural gas is the classic story. The use of classic stories has been customary for so long, and has recently come into such vogue again, that writers have forgotten their obligation to make the stories their own. They figure that the Aeschylean names will themselves establish the dignity and identity of the subject, while they – the modern adapters – get the credit and draw the royalties. They are not necessarily conscious opportunists. They probably assume, with some psychologists and anthropologists, that archetypal patterns of myth elicit profound responses of themselves, irrespective of presentation; if this were true, the poet would be unnecessary; it is a belief not to be discussed by a critic since the very fact of criticism presupposes its falsity. If we ask what difference it makes that Orin and Lavinia are versions of Orestes and Electra, the answer is that they thereby acquire an artificial prestige. They have become more important without any creative work on the author's part. We now associate them with the time-honored and sublime. They are inflated with cultural gas. It's like finding out that your girl friend is the daughter of a duke. If you are impressionable, you are impressed; she will seem different from now on, clad in all your illusions about nobility.

We are told that myth is useful because the audience knows the plot already and can turn its attention to the how and why. To this I would not protest that all adapters, including O'Neill, change the mythic plots, though this is true; what I have in mind is, rather, that they do not always change them enough. Events in their works have often no organic place there, they are fossilised vestiges of the older version. We ask: why does this character do that? And the answer is: because his Greek prototype did it. In *Mourning Becomes Electra* the myth makes it hard for O'Neill to let his people have their own identity at all, yet to the extent that they do have one, it is, naturally, a modern and American identity, and this in turn makes their ancient and Greek actions seem wildly improbable. Heaven knows that murders take place today as in ancient times; but the murders in O'Neill are not given today's reality.

Instead, the characters are blown up with psychological gas. O'Neill has boasted his ignorance of Freud, but such ignorance is not enough. He should be ignorant also of the watered-down Freudianism of Sardi's and the Algonquin,[1] the Freudianism of all those who are ignorant of Freud, the Freudianism of the sub-intelligentsia. It is through this Freudianism, and through it alone, that O'Neill has made the effort, though a vain one, to assimilate the myth to modern life. Now, what is it that your sub-intellectual knows about Freud? That he 'put everything down to sex'. Precisely; and that is what O'Neill does with the myth. Instead of reverent family feeling to unite an Orestes and an Electra we have incest. *Mourning Becomes Electra* is all sex talk. Sex *talk* – not sex lived and embodied, but sex talked of and fingered. The sex talk of the sub-intelligentsia. It is the only means by which some sort of eloquence and urgency gets into the play, the source of what is meant to be its poetry. The Civil War never gains the importance it might have had in this telling of the story, it is flooded out by sex. 'New England', surely a cultural conception with wider reference than this, stands only, in O'Neill, for the puritanic (that is, sexually repressive) attitude.

O'Neill is an acute case of what D. H. Lawrence called 'sex in the head'. Sex is almost the only idea he has – has insistently – and it is for him only an idea. Looking back on what I wrote about him a few years ago, I still maintain that O'Neill is no thinker. He is so little a thinker, it is dangerous for him to think. To prove this you have only to look at the fruits of his thinking; his comparatively thoughtless plays are better. For a non-thinker he thinks too much. Almost as bad as sex in the head is tragedy in the head, for tragedy too can decline into a doctrine and dwindle into an idea. And when the thing is absent, its 'idea' is apt to go soft. Tragedy is hard, but the idea of tragedy ('the tragic view of life', 'the tragic sense of life', and so forth) is seldom evoked without nostalgic longing. And the most decadent of longings is the longing for barbarism, *nostalgie de la boue*, such as is voiced by our tragedy-loving poets:

Poetry is not a civiliser, rather the reverse, for great poetry appeals to the most primitive instincts. . . . Tragedy has been regarded, ever since Aristotle, as a moral agent, a purifier of the mind and emotions. But the story of *Medea* is about a criminal adventurer and his gun-moll; it is no more moral than the story of Frankie and Johnny; only more ferocious. And so with the yet higher summits of Greek Tragedy, the Agamemnon series and the *Oedipus Rex*; they all tell primitive horror stories, and the conventional pious sentiments of the chorus are more than balanced by the bad temper and wickedness, or folly, of the principal characters. What makes them noble is the poetry; the poetry and the beautiful shapes of the plays, and the extreme violence born of extreme passion. . . . These are stories of disaster and death, and it is not in order to purge the mind of passions but because death and disaster are exciting. People love disaster, if it does not touch them too nearly – as we run to see a burning house or a motor crash. . . .

Aristotle's view of tragedy is humane; this one – that of Robinson Jeffers – is barbaric without the innocence of barbarism; it is neo-barbaric, decadent. O'Neill is too simple and earnest to go all the way with Jeffers. Puritanism and a rough-hewn honesty keep him within the realm of the human. But *Mourning Becomes Electra* does belong, so to speak, to the same world as Jeffers's remarks: a world that titillates itself with tragedy in the head. Your would-be tragedian despises realism, the problem play, liberalism, politics in general, optimism, and what not. Hence *Mourning Becomes Electra* is unrealistic, unsocial, illiberal, unpolitical and pessimistic. What of the *Oresteia*?

It celebrates the victory of law over arbitrary violence, of the community over the individual. It is optimistic, political, social, and with permissible licence it might be called liberal and realistic as well. *O tempora, O mores!* If one does not like O'Neill, it is not really he that one dislikes: it is our age – of which, like the rest of us, he is more the victim than the master.

SOURCE: extract from 'Trying to Like O'Neill' in *Kenyon Review*, 14 (July 1952); reproduced as ch. 9 in Bentley's *In Search of Theater* (New York, 1955), pp. 231–4. (For a further excerpting from Bentley's discussion, specific to *The Iceman Cometh*, see section 3 of Part Two, below.)

NOTE

1. [Ed] 'Sardi's' is a famous restaurant in New York's theatre district, where stage people and show-business celebrities meet, often to hear opening-night reviews. The Algonquin Hotel's 'round table' was a famous gathering-place of literary figures in the inter-war years.

Joseph Wood Krutch   'An Instinctive Perception
of Modern Tragedy'   (1932)

. . . As its title suggests, the fable follows, almost incident for incident, the main lines of the Greek story. Though O'Neill has set the action in New England just after the Civil War, his Clytemnestra murders Agamemnon and his Electra persuades Orestes to bring about the death of their common mother. Nor do such changes as are necessarily made in the motivation of the characters so much modify the effect of the story as merely restore that effect by translating the story into terms which we can fully comprehend. It is true that Electra loves her father and that Orestes loves his mother in a fashion which the Greeks either did not understand or, at least, did not specify. It is true also that the play implies that the psychological quirks responsible for the tragedy are the result of a conflict between puritanism and healthy love. But this is merely the way in which we understand such situations, and the fact remains that these things are *merely* implied, that the implications exist for the sake of the play, not the play for the sake of the implications. It is, moreover, this fact more than any other which indicates something very important in the nature of O'Neill's achievement. Hitherto most of our best plays have been – of necessity perhaps – concerned primarily with the exposition and defense of their intellectual or moral or psychological backgrounds. They have been written to demonstrate that it was legitimate to understand or judge men in the new ways characteristic of our time. But O'Neill has succeeded in writing a great play in which a reversal of this emphasis has taken place at last.

Because its thesis is taken for granted, it has no thesis. It is no more an exposition or defense of a modern psychological conception than Aeschylus is an exposition or defense of the tenets of the Greek religion, even though it does accept the one as Aeschylus accepts the other. It is on the other hand – and like all supremely great pieces of literature – primarily about the passions and primarily addressed to our interest in them. Once more we have a great play which does not 'mean' anything in the sense that the plays of Ibsen or Shaw or Galsworthy usually mean something, but one which does, on the contrary, mean the same thing that *Œdipus* and *Hamlet* and *Macbeth* mean – namely, that human beings are great and terrible creatures when they are in the grip of great passions, and that the spectacle of them is not only absorbing but also and at once horrible and cleansing.

Nineteenth-century critics of Shakespeare said that his plays were like the facts of nature, and though this statement has no intellectual content it does imply something concerning the attitude which we adopt toward *Mourning Becomes Electra* as well as toward Shakespeare. Our arguments and our analyses are unimportant so long as we attempt to discover in them the secret of our interest. What we do is merely to accept these fables as though they were facts and sit amazed by the height and the depth of human passions, by the grandeur and meanness of human deeds. No one knows exactly what it means to be 'purged by pity and terror', but for that very reason, perhaps, one returns to the phrase.

To find in the play any lack at all one must compare it with the very greatest works of dramatic literature, but when one does compare it with *Hamlet* or *Macbeth*, one realises that it does lack just one thing and that that thing is language – words as thrilling as the action which accompanies them. Take, for example, the scene in which Orin (Orestes) stands beside the bier of his father and apostrophises the body laid there. No one can deny that the speech is a good one, but what one desires with an almost agonising desire is something not merely good but something incredibly magnificent, something like 'Tomorrow and tomorrow and tomorrow . . .' or 'I could a tale unfold whose lightest word . . .'. If by some miracle such words could come, the situation would not be unworthy of them. Here is a scenario to which the most soaring eloquence and the most profound poetry are appropriate, and if it were granted us we should be swept aloft as no Anglo-Saxon audience since Shakespeare's time has had an opportunity to be. But no modern is capable of language really worthy of O'Neill's play, and the lack of that one thing is the penalty we must pay for living in an age which is not equal to more than prose. Nor is it to be supposed that I make this reservation merely for the purpose of saying that Mr O'Neill's play is not so good as the best of Shakespeare; I make it, on the contrary, in order to indicate where one must go in order to find a worthy comparison.

True tragedy may be defined as a dramatic work in which the outward failure of the principal personage is compensated for by the dignity and greatness of his character. But if this definition be accepted, then it must be recognised that the art of tragic writing was lost for many generations. Neither the frigid rhetorical exercises of the Victorians nor the sociological treaties of Ibsen and his followers are tragic in the true sense. The former lack the power to seem real enough to stir us deeply; the latter are too thoroughly pervaded by a sense of human littleness to be other than melancholy and dispiriting. O'Neill is almost alone among modern dramatic writers in possessing what appears to be an instinctive perception of what a modern tragedy would have to be.

Unlike the plays of 'literary' playwrights, his dramas have nothing archaic about them. They do not seek the support of a poetic faith in any of the conceptions which served the classical dramatists but are no longer valid for us. They are, on the contrary, almost cynically 'modern' in their acceptance of a rationalistic view of man and the universe. Yet he has created his characters upon so large a scale that their downfall is made once more to seem not merely pathetic, but terrible.

SOURCE: extract from the Introduction to *Nine Plays by Eugene O'Neill* (New York, 1932), pp. xix–xxii.

PART TWO

The Iceman Cometh

1. COMMENT BY O'NEILL

I 'I KNEW 'EM ALL ...' (October 1946)

...'I knew 'em all', he said. 'I've known 'em all for years.' His voice dropped gropingly into his remembrance of things past. 'All these people I have written about, I once knew.' Another long pause. 'I do not think that you can write anything of value or understanding about the present. You can only write about life if it is far enough in the past. The present is too much mixed up with superficial values; you can't know which thing is important and which is not.

'The past which I have chosen is one I knew. The man who owns this saloon, Harry Hope, and all the others – the Anarchists and Wobblies and French Syndicalists, the broken men, the tarts, the bartenders and even the saloon itself – are real. It's not just one place, perhaps, but it is several places that I lived in at one time or another' – he let his brooding eyes wander over the present living room, with its books and comfortable furniture, and his beloved collection of records neatly stacked on shelves – 'places I once knew put together in one.

'What have I done with this setting? Well, I've tried to show the inmates of Harry Hope's saloon there with their dreams. Some, you see, have just enough money from home to keep them going; but most of 'em keep from starving with the aid of the free lunch. This old Tammany politician who runs the place lives with his dreams, too, and he loves these people for he is one of them in his way.

'You ask, what is the significance, what do these people mean to us today? Well, all I can say is that it is a play about pipe dreams. And the philosophy is that there is always one dream left, one final dream, no matter how low you have fallen, down there at the bottom of the bottle. I know, because I saw it.'

... [The play's] philosophy is eternal and universal, O'Neill thinks: 'It will take man', he says, 'a million years to grow up and obtain a soul.'

O'Neill talked, too, about the title. To him titles are a matter of great importance.

'I always try to get into the title the surface meaning and at the same time the deeper significance.'

The surface meaning of *The Iceman Cometh* stems from a sardonic wisecrack, often repeated by one of the characters, who tells people he has left his wife safe at home with the iceman. The play revolves around this. But as it proceeds the 'iceman', who started as a ribald joke, takes on a different, deeper and even terrifying meaning and before the end becomes Death itself.

The idea for *Iceman* came to him suddenly. Because he knew all the characters so well there 'was not so much hard work as if I had had to dig them out'. Once started, the work 'flowed right along, page after page', he recalled, his deep eyes happy with the memory. Later he revised it once.

The Iceman Cometh apparently was created more easily than others of his plays. 'I don't just write plays', he explained. 'I make many notes over a long period. Then I write a scenario of 20,000 or so words. I draw out all the scenes from my own strange conception of perspective, which I understand, even if directors don't always.'. . .

SOURCE: extract from Karl Schriftgriesser's 'Interview with O'Neill', in *New York Times* ('Sunday Drama Section', 6 Oct. 1946), pp. 1, 3.

II   'PERSONALLY, I LOVE IT'   (AUGUST 1940)

Many thanks for your letter regarding *The Iceman Cometh*. I'm damned pleased you like it. Personally, I love it! And I'm sure my affection is not wholly inspired by nostalgia for the dear dead days 'on the bottom of the sea', either! I have a confident hunch that this play, as drama, is one of the best things I've ever done. In some ways, perhaps *the* best. What I mean is, there are moments in it that suddenly strip the secret soul of a man stark naked, not in cruelty or moral superiority, but with an understanding compassion which sees him as a victim of the ironies of life and of himself. Those moments are for me the depth of tragedy, with nothing more that can possibly be said. . . .

SOURCE: extract from letter to Lawrence Langner (11 Aug. 1940); quoted in Langner's *The Magic Curtain* (New York, 1951), p. 398.

III   'THEY DO IT. THEY HAVE TO'   (DECEMBER 1940)

. . . I'm delighted *The Iceman Cometh* made such a deep impression on you. I was confident it would. And I'm grateful for your frank

critical suggestions. I wanted them, and will keep them in mind
when it is time to give the play a final going over, which it hasn't
had yet. I know when this is done I will find that a general pruning
is needed, but I'm sure I won't agree with you on the advisability
of any drastic condensation of the first part. I see what you're
driving at, but I honestly believe if I did it you would be the first to
see afterward it was wrong because it had changed the essential
character and unique quality of the play. After all, what I've tried
to write is a play where at the end you feel you know the souls of
the seventeen men and women who appear – and the women who
don't appear – as well as if you'd read a play about each of them. I
couldn't condense much without taking a lot of life from some of
these people and reducing them to lay figures. You would find if I
did not build up the complete picture of the group as it now is in
the first part – the atmosphere of the place, the humour and
friendship and human warmth and *deep inner contentment* of the
bottom – you would not be so interested in these people and you
would find the impact of what follows a lot less profoundly disturbing.
You wouldn't feel the same sympathy and understanding for them,
or be so moved by what Hickey does to them.

It's hard to explain exactly my intuitions about this play. Perhaps
I can put it best by saying *The Iceman Cometh* is something I want to
make life reveal about itself, fully and deeply and roundly – that it
takes place for me in life not in a theatre – that the fact it is a play
which can be produced with actors is secondary and incidental to
me and even, quite unimportant – and so it would be a loss to me
to sacrifice anything of the complete life for the sake of stage and
audience

That doesn't say it, but never mind. You'll get what I mean.
Take for example your point about the part near the end where
each character tells his face-saving version of his experience when
he went out to confront his pipe dream. *I* don't write this as a piece
of playwrighting. *They do it. They have to.* Each of them! In just that
way! It is tragically, pitifully important to them to do this! They
must tell these lies as a first step in taking up life again. Moreover,
their going through with this pathetic formula heightens by contrast
the tension of Larry's waiting for the sound of Parritt hurtling down
to the backyard, and the agony he goes through. If our American
acting and directing cannot hold this scene up without skimping it,
then to hell with our theatre! You know as well as I that the direction
and acting of the old Moscow Art Theatre, or Kamerny, could
sustain the horrible contrast and tension of this episode and make
it one of the most terrible scenes in the play, as it is to me now. . . .

SOURCE: extract from letter to Kenneth Macgowan (30 Dec. 1940); reproduced in Jackson R. Bryer (ed.), *The Theatre We Worked For: The Letters of Eugene O'Neill to Kenneth Macgowan* (New Haven, Conn., 1982), pp. 256–7.

IV   'A BIG KIND OF COMEDY'   (SEPTEMBER 1946)

. . . Decades ahead of his day, O'Neill said cautionary things at the press conference [at the Theatre Guild offices on 2 Sept.] that would be accepted as gospel among the more thoughtful in the 1960s and 1970s; but in 1946, with the national mood one of confidence and optimism over our emergence as the predominant power from the most catastrophic war in history, he stood an isolated Jeremiah. Voicing some of his central thinking when asked about the theme of his nine-play Cycle, he declared that he considered America, 'instead of being the most successful country in the world, is its greatest failure . . . the greatest failure because it was given every-thing, more than any other country. Through moving as rapidly as it has, it has never acquired any real roots. Its main idea is that everlasting game of trying to possess your own soul and the things outside of it, too.'

He kept rubbing his trembly hands, folding and unfolding them constantly; his attitude toward his tremor, he said, was one of 'enraged resignation'. At times his voice almost died in his throat, but now and then, in his effort to speak up, it suddenly filled the room with a booming bass. He sensed, he said, 'a feeling around, or I'm mistaken, of fate. Kismet, the negative fate; not in the Greek sense. . . . It's struck me as time goes on, how something funny, even farcical, can suddenly without any apparent reason, break up into something gloomy and tragic. . . . A sort of unfair *non sequitur*, as though events, as though life, were being manipulated just to confuse us; a big kind of comedy that doesn't stay funny very long. I've made some use of it in *The Iceman*. The first act is hilarious comedy, *I think*, but then some people may not even laugh. At any rate, the comedy breaks up and the tragedy comes on.' . . .

SOURCE: extract from Louis Sheaffer, *O'Neill: Son and Artist* (Boston, Mass., 1973), pp. 577–8. Sheaffer here reports extensively on the 'mass interview' O'Neill gave to the press on 2 September 1946 – this being the means the dramatist devised to deal with 'many individual requests' for personal interviews about the play.

2. COMMENTATORS ON THE 1946 & LATER PRODUCTIONS

Brooks Atkinson   (1946)

'The Heart and Wonder of a Poet'

Mr O'Neill has written one of his best plays. Dipping back into his memory thirty-four years, reaching down to the tatterdemalions of a mouldy bar-room, he has come up with a dark and somber play that compares with the best work of his earliest period. *The Iceman Cometh*, he calls it to no one's satisfaction but his own, and it was acted with rare insight and vitality at the Martin Beck [Theatre] last evening. Writing it for a performance that lasts more than four hours is a sin that rests between Mr O'Neill and his Maker. Long plays have become nothing more than a bad label with our first dramatist.

But if that is the way Mr O'Neill wants to afflict harmless play-goers, let us accept our fate with nothing more than a polite demur. For the only thing that matters is that he has plunged again into the black quagmire of man's illusions and composed a rigadoon of death as strange and elemental as his first works. Taking his characters again out of the lower depths, as he did in the 'S. S. Glencairn' series, he is looking them over with bleak and mature introspection. And like all his best work, this one is pre-eminently actable. The Theatre Guild performance, under Eddie Dowling's direction, is a masterpiece of tones, rhythms and illumination.

The whisky-ridden derelicts who drag their broken carcasses through Harry Hope's bar came out of O'Neill's youth when he, too, was drinking too much and dreaming of becoming a writer. They are men whose only lives are illusions – 'pipe dreams', O'Neill calls their memories which they foolishly translate into hopes for a future that will never exist. When the play opens they are happily living together in a spirit of human rancor, broken, tired and drunken but buoyed up by romantic illusions about themselves.

What shatters their stupor is the arrival of an old comrade who has reformed. he has found peace at last, he says. He does not need whisky any more, he says, because he has purged himself of illusions and knows the full truth of himself. Instead of making them happy, however, his reform movement destroys their decaying contentment. Without illusions, they find themselves standing alone and terrified. They cannot face the hollowness of themselves without the opium of illusions. But they are released in the last act by the awful discovery that their teacher has freed himself from illusions by committing a crime that will sit him in the electric chair. He is free from illusions because he has resigned from life and is already dead in spirit. Whereupon, the derelicts drink up again and happily relapse into the stupor of the bottle.

That is the abstract story of *The Iceman Cometh*. But the concrete drama on the stage is infinitely more flavorsome. Among its battered wretches it includes a raffish lot of social outcasts in amazing variety – an IWW[1] emigré, a broken gambler, a cop who was thrown off the force, a British infantry officer who stole regimental funds, a Boer commando leader who showed the white feather, the well-educated son of an embezzler, some prostitutes and bar-keeps. The Lord knows they talk too much, for Mr O'Neill insists on grinding their bitterness into very small and precise pieces. But it is good talk – racy, angry, comic drumbeats on the lid of doom, and a strong undercurrent of elemental drama silently washes the gloomy charnel-house where they sit waiting.

Surely it is no accident that most of Mr O'Neill's plays act well. Although he seems on the surface to be a literal writer, interminably fussing over minor details, his best plays move across the stage as methodically and resolutely as a heavy battle attack, and over-run strategic points with a kind of lumbering precision. The performance of *The Iceman Cometh* ranks among the theatre's finest works. To house these rags and tags of the human race, Robert Edmond Jones has created a mean and dingy last refuge that nevertheless glows with an articulate meaning, like a Daumier print, as one alert spectator observed.

To anyone who loves acting, Dudley Digges' performance as the tottering and irascible saloon proprietor is worth particular cherishing. Although the old man is half dead, Mr Digges' command of the actor's art of expressing character and theme is brilliantly alive; it overflows with comic and philosophical expression. As the messenger of peace, James Barton is also superb – common, unctuous, cheerful and fanatical; and Mr Barton reads one of the longest speeches on record without letting it drift off into sing-song or monotony.

As the bar-room's master of cosmic thinking, Carl Benton Reid is vigorously incisive, and lends substance to the entire performance.

Nicholas Joy is giving the best performance of his career as the unfrocked captain. As the garrulous night bartender, Tom Pedi with his querulous vitality streaks an amusing ribbon of color throughout the drama. There are also notable performances by John Marriott, as the discredited gambler; Paul Crabtree, as an IWW traitor; and E. G. Marshall, as a fallen Harvard man.

If there were any justice in the world, all the actors would get a line of applause here. But this bulletin, like Mr O'Neill's play, is already much too garrulous. Let us cut it short with one final salute to a notable drama by a man who writes with the heart and wonder of a poet.

SOURCE: review ('Mr O'Neill's New Work with Four-Hour Running Time Has Its World Premiere') of the opening performance at the Martin Beck Theatre, 9 October 1946, in the *New York Times* (10 Oct. 1946)

NOTE

1. [Ed.] IWW – Industrial Workers of the World – was a militant syndicalist section in organised labour in the United States in the years before the First World War. It opposed political and trade union 'reformism', advocating and promoting revolutionary industrial activity. Its main support came from ill-paid immigrant workers.

George Jean Nathan   (1946)

'The Tragedy that is Death in Life'

With the appearance of this long-awaited work, our theatre has become dramatically alive again. It makes most of the plays of other American playwrights produced during the more than twelve-year period of O'Neill's absence look comparatively like so much damp tissue paper. In it there is an understanding of the deeper elements of human nature, a comprehension of the confused instincts that make up the life of mortals, and an evocation of pity for the tortured existence of dazed mankind that not merely most but all of those plays in combination have not faintly suggested. It is, in short, one of the best of its author's works and one that again firmly secures his position not only as the first of American dramatists but, with Shaw and O'Casey, one of the three really distinguished among the world's living.

These, I appreciate, are big words and probably contributive to the suspicion that their inditer has foregone his old Pyrrhonism.[1] They are also doubtless obnoxious and challenging to such persons as either resent what seems to be extravagant praise at the expense of other playwrights or are constitutionally averse to superlatives of any kind and ready to throw off their coats if anyone has the gall to say even that Bach was the greatest composer who ever lived or that horseradish sauce is the best of all things to go with boiled beef. But the words, I believe, are none the less in good order. If they are not and if the play is not what I think it is, I am prepared to atone for my ignorance by presenting gratis to anyone who can offer convincing contrary evidence the complete bound works of all our American playwrights from Bronson Howard through Charles Klein, David Belasco and Augustus Thomas down to the geniuses responsible for *Joan of Lorraine*, *Another Part of the Forest*, *Dream Girl* and *Maid in the Ozarks*.

Laying hold of an assortment of social outcasts quartered in a disreputable saloon on the fringe of New York in the year 1912 and introducing into their drunken semblance of contentful hope an allergy in the shape of a Werlean[2] travelling salesman, O'Neill distils from them, slowly but inexorably, the tragedy that is death in life. Superficially at times suggesting a cross between Gorky's *The Lower Depths* and Saroyan's *The Time of Your Life*, let alone Ibsen's *The Wild Duck*, the play with its author's uncommon dramaturgical skill gradually weaves its various vagrant threads into a solid thematic pattern and in the end achieves a purge and mood of compassion that mark it apart from the bulk of contemporary drama. There are repetitions in the middle sections which O'Neill has deemed necessary to the impact of the play but which in this opinion might be got rid of with no loss. There is also still an excess of profanity, for all the author's liberal cutting, that becomes disturbing to any ear that gags at such facile over-emphasis. And since the uncut version of *Hamlet*, which is a good play too, can be played in its entirety in little more than three and a half hours, the longer running time of *The Iceman Cometh* may seem to some, and quite rightly, not only superfluous but a little pretentious. Yet small matter. In the whole history of drama there has been only one really perfect tragedy – incidentally, only one-third as long – and, while this of O'Neill's is scarcely to be compared with it, it still rises far above its possible errors.

With a few nimble strokes, O'Neill pictures vividly the innards of even the least of his variegated characters, from the one-time circus grifter to the one-time police lieutenant, from the quondam boss of a Negro gambling den to the erstwhile Boer War correspondent, and from the night and the day bartenders and the wreck of a college graduate to the former editor of Anarchist magazines and the old captain once in the British armed services. Only in the characters of his three street-walkers does he work rather obviously; truthfully, perhaps, but in a theatrically routine manner. Yet in his major figures – Slade, the one-time Syndicalist-Anarchist, Hickey, the hardware salesman, Hope, the proprietor of the saloon, etc. – the hand is as steady and sure as ever.

The long monologue, only now and then momentarily interrupted, wherein toward the drama's conclusion the salesman relates the relief from himself secured by the murder of his wife, is one of the most impressive pieces of writing in contemporary dramatic literature: emotionally searching and definitely moving. The relations of Slade and the young man with memory of his betrayed mother on his agonised conscience are manoeuvred with high suspensive dexterity, even if at one or two points to the hypercritical slightly overplanted. The dialogue throughout is driving; there is robust humor to alleviate the atmospheric sordidness; and out of the whole emerge in no small degree the profound essences of authentic tragedy.

In the author's own analysis of his play as he has confided it to me the dominant intention has been a study in the workings of strange friendship. That intention, it is not to be gainsaid, has been fully realised. But as I read the script and see it in stage action, it seems to me that, far above and beyond it, there rises the theme of the tragedy which lies in bogus self-substantiation and the transient, pitiable satisfaction which it bequeaths. That, however, is the play's virtue: to different men it may convey different things. But to all with any emotional understanding and to all with any appreciation of the drama it must convey the satisfaction of a theatre that, if only for a short while, has again come into its rightful own.

In a setting by Robert Edmond Jones which catches perfectly the atmosphere of the play and with lighting that alternately gives the stage and groupings the effect of Daumier and George Bellows, Eddie Dowling, with many acceptable critical suggestions from the author, has accomplished an impressive example of direction. In only two or three details has he missed, and the fault in those cases was scarcely his. O'Neill's men's toilet to the far left of the stage with the 'This Is It' sign is gratuitous, since it is strangely, even phenomenally, never once used by any of the hard-drinking denizens of the saloon and it thus serves no purpose and is simply a gesture in juvenile waggery. Dowling's idea that it be given some small justification by installing Hugo Kalmar, the drooling Anarchist editor, in it at one point and having him declaim his parrot lines from its interior – an excellent comedy touch that would have suited the action with no slightest violation of the text – was vetoed by O'Neill. The play's ending, which presently goes a little flat, might also, as Dowling wished, have been inspirited if – as counterpoint to Slade's final 'Be God, I'm the only real convert to death Hickey made here; from the bottom of my coward's heart I mean that now!', – the drunken singing and wild pounding on the table by the assembled, happily unredeemed bibuli had not been cut by the author and had been moved a bit forward from its place in the original script. And if the director had been allowed to lend a greater touch of his familiar 'mood' staging to the play, which he was not, the spirit of the drama would have been materially aided.

Except for James Barton's reading of the extended monologue, which is so fumblingly and poorly done that it disastrously drops the drama at its most important point (the rôle should have been played by Dowling himself; he could do nothing, he found, to alter Barton's method), along with Carl Benton Reid's minstrel-show-interlocutor Slade, the performances from first to last are admirable, in particular those of Dudley Digges, Morton L. Stevens, Nicholas Joy, Russell Collins, Tom Pedi (who is superb as the Italian bartender-pimp) and Paul Crabtree. In all, to repeat, a drama wrought brilliantly out of the time-honored theme of man's pitiable necessity for illusion and played for the most part, at least up to a few minutes of its final curtain, in the true manner of real theatre.

O'Neill is the only dramat'st in the history of the American theatre who has achieved real world status. His plays have been produced in most of the civilised countries of the globe; he has been awarded the Nobel prize for the body of his work; he has been the subject of critical discussion in South America, England, Germany, France, Italy, Greece, Russia, the Scandinavian lands, the Balkans, Australia, Japan and China. Almost as much has been written about him as about one-half all the living playwrights rolled together. Only Shaw has consumed more space.

In the United States, South America, France, Italy, Russia, the Scandinavian countries, Rumania, Greece, Australia, Japan and China, the critical attitude toward him in the main has been extremely favourable. In Germany, when criticism was operating freely, it was, with a few exceptions, highly appreciative. In England alone has there most often been either a luke-warm or chilly attitude toward him. . . .

SOURCE: extract from review essay on the Theatre Guild production, 1946, in *The Theatre Book of the Year, 1946–49* (New York, 1947), pp. 93–7.

NOTES

1. [Ed.] Pyrrhonism: the philosophical position of Pyrrho (c.360–270 BC), reputedly the originator of absolute scepticism.
2. [Ed.] Werlean: an allusion to Gregers Werle, the destructive idealist in Ibsen's *The Wild Duck*.

José Quintero   (1957)

Postscript to a Journey: 1956 Production, New York

On 15 March 1956, I went to see Carlotta Monterey O'Neill for the first time, to discuss a possible revival of her late husband's tragedy, *The Iceman Cometh*.

The Circle in the Square Theatre, of which I am director and one of the producers, had been yearning to do a work by Eugene O'Neill for a long time. But whenever we made inquiries we always met the same answer: 'All the works of Mr O'Neill, are, at the moment, not available for production.' Mrs O'Neill's invitation to call seemed promising, and I was a hopeful, if anxious, visitor. I was frightened and nervous, for my hostess was, after all, the widow of America's greatest dramatist. It was a remarkable and, as it turned out, a portentous meeting. I saw a lady of medium height, her black hair pulled back and cut short at the back of the neck. The dark penetrating eyes were arresting in the steadiness of their gaze. She was dressed in black, which she wore with distinction.

She began to talk about her husband's work, almost as though he were present, as in a sense he was. There were pictures of Eugene O'Neill everywhere. Pictures of him when he was a young, lean, handsome man. Other pictures when pain and anger and frustration had given his eyes a terrifying look. Pictures of Mr and Mrs O'Neill taken on their honeymoon in Paris. In the bookcases there were three or four copies of every one of his plays. Mrs O'Neill talked of his dedication to his work, and how work was the only thing that he really cared about. She asked me a few questions about the Circle in the Square, and I answered them. She rose from her chair and said, 'You can do *The Iceman Cometh*'. I left the apartment, almost believing that permission to do the play had come from the dead dramatist himself.

It was less a permission than a sacred charge. *The Iceman Cometh* presented enormous problems at the Circle. It has a cast of twenty, and almost every role is highly complex. The central part of Hickey the salesman, is one of the longest and most difficult in American theatre literature. Where was our little theatre going to get all of those people . . . on so stringently limited a budget? We sent out a casting call and began listening to actors, 100 to 125 a day. After four weeks we had cast all of the characters – with the exception of Hickey. It was an oddly assorted and most unorthodox cast, ranging from highly trained and experienced actors to ones who were beginning their careers at the age of fifty. Some of them had never been in a play before.

The impossible problem remained: We needed a great actor who would be willing to play for $30 a week. That was when Jason Robards, Jnr came into our lives. I had called him, really, with a lesser role in mind, but he insisted on reading a section of Hickey's big speech at the end of the play. (He later told me that he had needed a couple of drinks to make such a demand.)

We had found the impossible. We had found the actor for Hickey.

My approach in directing *The Iceman Cometh* was different from that used in any play I had ever done. It had to be, for this was not built as an orthodox play. It resembles a complex musical form, with themes repeating themselves with slight variation, as melodies do in a symphony. It is a valid device, though O'Neill has often been criticised for it by those who do not see the strength and depth of meaning the repetition achieves.

My work was somewhat like that of an orchestra conductor, emphasising rhythms, being constantly aware of changing tempos; every character advanced a different theme. The paradox was that for the first time as a director, I began to understand the meaning of precision in drama – and it took a play four and one-half hours long to teach me, a play often criticised as rambling and overwritten.

We rehearsed four weeks and our opening took place on the afternoon of 8 May 1956. We didn't know then, of course, what the critics and the public would think; but at the end of that first performance we, all of us, had a sense of one important success; that a great play had won the right to be revaluated.

Source: article, 'Postscript to a Journey', *Theatre Arts*, XLI (April 1957), pp. 27–9, 88.

Brooks Atkinson   (1956)

'A Mighty Theatre Work': 1956 Production, New York

Since José Quintero's productions at Circle in the Square are always admirable, no one should be surprised by his latest achievement.

But it is impossible not to be excited by his production of Eugene O'Neill's *The Iceman Cometh*, which opened in Mr Quintero's theatre yesterday. It is a major production of a major theatre work. Taking a long script with a massive theme, Mr Quintero has succeeded in bringing every part of it alive in the theatre. Although he tells the story simply and spontaneously, he leaves no doubt about the value he places on O'Neill's place in the literature of the stage. Mr Quintero seems to take him on the level of Ibsen, Strindberg, Gorky and other modern masters of tragic writing.

If *The Iceman Cometh* seems to belong in Mr Quintero's theatre, there is a good reason. For Circle in the Square was a night-club originally, and all four of the acts of the O'Neill drama are set in a saloon. The audience has the sensation of participating. The rows of seats are only an extension of David Hays' setting of the battered, blowzy waterfront saloon and flophouse that is under the fabulous proprietorship of Harry Hope. A few tables and chairs, a squalid bar, a flimsy door leading into the street, a handful of fly-blown chandeliers and a few ranks of benches for the audience – they are all part of the same setting and closely related on that account.

In the circumstances, it is difficult to be objective about this melancholy, sardonic drama that pulls the rug from under the whole structure of life. It seems, not like something written, but like something that is happening. Although it is terrible in its comment on the need for illusions to maintain an interest in life, it is also comic. Some of the dialogue is pretty funny. On the surface, all the characters are comic, since they live in a world of befuddled fantasy and talk big to compensate for the puniness of their spirits.

But beneath them there is nothing more substantial than a void of blackness. These are creatures that once were men – very pungent and picturesque creatures, too, for O'Neill was a good deal of a romantic. But the tone of *The Iceman Cometh* is devastatingly tragic. Life is bearable, it seems to say, only when men contrive not to look at the truth.

The performance lasts four and three-quarter hours. For *The Iceman Cometh* is one of the O'Neill marathon dramas. No doubt it could be cut and compressed without destroying anything essential. But as a creative work by a powerful writer, it is entitled to its excesses, which, in fact, may account for the monumental feeling of doom that it pulls down over the heads of the audience.

The performance is a vital one. Mr Quintero is a versatile conductor who knows how to vary his attack with changes in volume and rhythm; he knows how to orchestrate a performance. In one important respect, this performance surpasses the original of ten years ago. Jason Robards, Jnr plays Hickey, the catalyst in the narrative, like an evangelist. His unction, condescension and piety introduce an element of moral affection that clarifies the perspective of the drama as a whole. His heartiness, his aura of good fellowship give the character of Hickey a feeling of evil mischief it did not have before.

In both the writing and the acting, *The Iceman Cometh* is a mighty theatre work. O'Neill is a giant, and Mr Quintero is a remarkably gifted artist.

SOURCE: review of the Circle in the Square production's opening performance, 8 May 1956, in the *New York Times* (9 May 1956).

Kenneth Tynan   (1958)

'A Wonderfully Worrying Evening': 1958 London Production

Paul Valéry once defined the true snob as a man who was afraid to admit that he was bored when he was bored; and he would be a king of snobs indeed who failed to admit to a *mauvais quart d'heure* about half-way through *The Iceman Cometh*. But perhaps, as a colleague suggests, all great art should be slightly boring. A vast structure is to be built, and in the long process there are bound to be moments of tedium: they are the price we pay for size and splendour, and we pay it gladly once the architect has convinced us that we can trust him. O'Neill convinced last Wednesday's audience in thirty minutes flat, after which no doubts remained. This was no crank, planning a folly dependent on sky-hooks: we were safe in the hands of the American theatre's nearest counterpart to Frank Lloyd Wright.

But how did he hold us in our seats through four hours and more of circular alcoholic conversation? By means of verbal magic? I think not. O'Neill writes clumsily and top-heavily. He never achieves the luminous, crystallising phrase, nor has he the opposite virtue of earthy authenticity: his gin-mill dialogue has the stagey swagger of melodrama. If it isn't the language, then, is it the universality of the theme? Again, no. Most of the characters are special cases, confirmed alcoholics out of touch with any kind of reality that cannot be bottled. When Hickey, the reformed drunk, urges these red-eyed wet-brains to abandon their pipe-dreams and face the truth about themselves, we know that the cure will kill them; but we cannot relate this knowledge to our own lives as we can, for instance, when Gregers Werle strips Ekdal of his illusions in *The Wild Duck*. Many of us, like Ekdal, have a dark-room of the soul where we develop dreams that the light of day would obliterate. But very few of us actually live in the dark-room, so enslaved to our fantasies that we would rather have DTS than give them up.

No, what holds us about the play is the insight it gives us into O'Neill himself. It is a dramatised neurosis, with no holds barred, written in a vein of unsparing, implacable honesty. 'Speak, that I may see thee', said Ben Jonson; and when O'Neill speaks, he hides nothing. Instead of listening to a story, we are shaking hands with a man, and a man whose vision of life is as profoundly dark as any since Aeschylus. It is this autobiographical intensity that grips us throughout the *longueurs* of the narrative and the gawkiness (I had almost said Gorkiness) of the style. For O'Neill, a pipe-dream is not just one alternative to despair: it is the only alternative. His barroom derelicts comfort and sustain one another as long as each tolerates the other's illusions. Once Hickey has removed the illusions, nothing remains but guilt and mutual accusation. One may not agree with O'Neill's conclusions, but one cannot escape the look in his eye, which is as magnetic as the Ancient Mariner's. He speaks like a man who has touched bottom himself; for whom words like 'inferior' no longer have meaning. He is one of the few writers who can enter, without condescension or contempt, the world of those whom the world has rejected.

The play demands and gets superb direction. Peter Wood's production is better in many respects than the New York version I saw and admired last spring. Like all good directors, Mr Wood is loyal to the text; he is also constructively disloyal to the hysterical punctuation and overheated stage-directions of which American playwrights are so fond. His cast deserves individual attention. Nicholas Meredith plays a cashiered Blimp, making a character out of a caricature by discreet understatement; Lee Montague is funny, dour and truthful as an Italian bar-keep who cannot bring himself to admit that he is also a pimp; and Jack MacGowran, pinch-faced and baggy-trousered, plays the tetchy proprietor with a weasel brilliance I have not seen since the heyday of F. J. McCormick. In the sketchily written role of a drunken Harvard alumnus, Michael Bryant gets closer to the raw nerve of reality than any West End débutant I can remember. The pale, shaky smile, the carefully preserved sophistication, the glib, hectic delivery all converge to make a rounded, original whole, half clown, half martyr.

Of the three characters, Patrick Magee does not quite get the rock-sombre melancholy of Larry, the disgusted nihilist who has deserted anarchism for drink; but the other two are perfect – Vivian Matalon as a guilty young stool-pigeon, pathetically ripe for suicide; and Ian Bannen as Hickey, the manic salesman, driving his friends to destruction with the enthusiasm of a revivalist. I winced a bit at the Kensington cosiness of Mr Wood's three waterfront tarts. Otherwise, the production is flawless. It makes a wonderfully worrying evening. . . .

SOURCE: extract from double-review (with Tennessee Williams's *Cat on a Hot Tin Roof*) of the Arts Theatre production's opening performance, 29 January 1958, in the *Observer* (2 Feb. 1958); reproduced in Tynan's *A View of the English Stage, 1944–63* (London, 1975), pp. 208–10.

Frederick C. Wilkins   (1985)

'An Experience to Cherish': 1985 Production, New York

The milk has been spilled and there is no efficacy in tears. The monumental revival of Quintero's legendary 1956 production of *Iceman*, reuniting three members of that earlier production – Jason Robards (Hickey), José Quintero (director) and James Greene (Jimmy Tomorrow) – certainly deserved a much longer run, and would have had it if theatre-going were still the serious activity it once was on the Great White Way. Unfortunately, today's audiences want something light, splashy, and preferably tuneful: something that will tax neither their patience nor their minds. (If your message is about 'tomorrow' being 'always a day away', you'd best have it sung by a gaggle of cuddly urchins or risk precipitous unemployment!) But even a short-lived O'Neill revival is cause for rejoicing, and a production as lovingly crafted as this one quickly stills all bitterness at its inhospitable rejection by the general public. One can only hope that a tape or film was made before the closing, to provide future generations with a record of how moving and exhilarating *Iceman* can be when both the letter and the spirit of the text are brought to life by artists of genius. . . .

Admittedly, at moments of stasis, when the denizens of Harry Hope's saloon had not been roiled by the two intruders, Hickey and Parritt, the pace was slow. But life *is* slow at the bottom of the sea. The audience must imbibe the group's ordinary atmosphere, and at length, before the peaceful depths are agitated by outsiders. You cannot understand the boredom in Chekhov's country houses without experiencing a little of that boredom yourself; and you cannot understand the threat that Hickey poses to the hopeless hopers at Harry's until you have shared a table there in the dim, slow light of early dawn. O'Neill knew what he was doing, and José Quintero honored that intent admirably, offering no cute, distracting 'business' as each individual voice was slowly added to the accumulating chord of communality. (To shift metaphors: the long opening scene is a still-life, and the stillness offers an important clue to the life. How ironic that the play's first words – Rocky's to Larry as he offers him a drink – are 'Make it fast'! The playwright's tacit injunction to the director is quite the opposite, and Quintero had the faith in his master to 'make it slow'.)

Ben Edwards' unit set filled the wide, shallow stage of the Lunt-Fontanne: bar area at the right, coldly lighted (at the start) through the establishment's massive but greasy and fogged front window; back room at the left, more warmly lighted through a small window downstage of an old upright piano. The rear wall jutted out slightly at the middle, between the two areas, to give the suggestion of a division. And the inhabitants were slumped, in varying postures of sodden indolence, at tables scattered across the whole expanse of the stage. As was true of the direction, all was realistic but spare: there was no row of vari-colored bottles behind the towering mahogany bar, no period gewgaws to tickle the memories of old timers and distract from the human detritus on display in this subaqueous realm that seemed so real for all its sparseness. The initial tableau – rightly praised by Frank Rich in the *New York Times* (24 November 1985) – with its suggestions of peace and death, remained etched in the mind, and neither the disruptions caused by Hickey's 'mission', nor the sad attempts at party decoration in Act Two, could erase it. . . .

Donald Moffat, his head usually in his hands, and his sad, red-rimmed eyes shadowed by thick white brows, caught both the gruff and tender sides of Larry Slade, increasingly uncomfortable in his seat in an illusory grandstand as he is needled into ending the misery of a boy who may very well be his son. That son, Don Parritt, must be the most thankless role in the play. A self-peeling onion who reveals lie after lie about his actions until reaching the final truth inside, he has little chance of earning much sympathy. Sometimes sympathy is sought by casting a matinee-idol type – like Robert Redford or Jeff Bridges – in the part. No such sentimentality was attempted this time: Paul McCrane, short, slick-haired and crammed into an ill-fitting suit, had all the romantic charisma of a stoat, and his selection for the part was uniformly panned by reviewers. But I felt that his edgy, shrill performance was just right: to pity Don Parritt because he is a cute-kid-gone-wrong would be to engage in 'the wrong kind of pity'. If Parritt is to be pitied, it must not be on the basis of looks or manner. This production did not settle for easy answers, and Mr McCrane deserves credit for taking the knocks attendant on that brave decision.

Of course, any performance of *The Iceman Cometh* stands or falls on the basis of its Hickey – as was so sadly revealed in the 1973 film: a delicious doughnut with a gaping hole in the middle. And no performer has ever been as associated with the role as Jason Robards Jnr, who starred in the 1956 production and later recreated his performance on television. But more than a quarter century has passed since those ventures, and one wondered if he could do it again, so much later. The answer is yes and no: he did it again, and brilliantly; but he did it differently, finding new depths in the part that more than compensated for any diminution of brio that the passage of time necessarily entails. From his arrival song, though it was delivered to a jaunty dance step that showed why he was so loved by his former associates, this was a Hickey who was spent – spent by age, and spent by a guilt that cannot be buck-and-winged away or hidden beneath the sheeny black of his hair. (Whether we were meant to infer that Hickey had had some tonsorial doing-up en route to the party, I'm not sure; but the ebon hair lent him a cadaverous look that can't have been unintentional, especially as it was shared by at least two of his converts – Harry and Jimmy – when he sent them out on their missions of truth.) . . . Not that performer or character was listless: the quick smile, the glad hand, the dancing and frequent movement seemed as real as the energy behind them. But when this Hickey succumbed to sleep late in the first act, it was especially believable.

No one could equal Robards in the sardonic thrust of his grinning accusations of others' illusions: this is no friend to have around if you've got a mask to keep in place. And no one will ever better his harrowing delivery of the last-act monologue – though I didn't think his banging on the piano keys at 'bitch' – the last word of his remembered remark to Evelyn – did anything to enhance the speech's, and the play's, most climactic moment. The moment's force is verbal; it got the delivery for which Mr Robards is rightly famed; and a piano chord, even a cacophonous one, added nothing. Robards' performance was studded with moments of brilliance: his prophetic refusal to shake Parritt's hand when they are introduced in Act One (somehow he's 'on to' this soul-mate from the start); his looming presence when, unseen by the others, he overhears Larry's comments about him in Act Two; the electric moment at the party when, after proposing a toast to Harry, he rises to a pitch of evangelical fervor –

This peace is real! – It's a fact! – I know! – Because I've got it! – Right – here – in – front – of – you!

– the grimace of pain in Act Three, when he realises the failure of his attempt at salvation for all; and the obsessive turning of his wedding ring during the last-act monologue, which was delivered with enough erratic, kinetic movement to make clear that the peace he's claimed to have achieved is as illusory as any of the others' pipe dreams.

I must say that I found myself resenting the other characters' interruptions of the monologue – except, of course, for the Parritt counterpoint, which is essential. But my quarrel there is with the playwright, who might have trusted the actors to reveal, by face and gesture, their reactions. Surely he knew, even if they don't, that they are interrupting one of the greatest speeches in modern drama!

Since I've already quarrelled with the playwright, I might as well mention my one additional displeasure – with the theatre. *Iceman*, as I've said in the past, requires a closeness between performers and spectators to achieve its full force; and the Lunt-Fontanne is a huge, deep, high-staged playhouse that defies the establishment of that closeness. However much empathy the actors arouse, our physical distance from them tends to diffuse it. There is no way of knowing, of course, but I'd bet that if the production had taken place on a thrust-stage, like that at the Circle in the Square, it would still be running. Would that it were!

These few reservations notwithstanding, the 1985 production of *The Iceman Cometh* was an experience to cherish. To Messrs Robards and Quintero – indeed, to all – a hearty hurrah. I doubt that we shall see their like again.

104 FREDERICK C. WILKINS (1985)

SOURCE: extracts from review in the *Eugene O'Neill Newsletter* (Winter, 1985), pp. 23–5, 28, of the American National Theatre production at the Lunt-Fontanne Theatre, 29 Sept.–1 Dec. 1985. Wilkins attended the performance on Thursday 17 Oct. (The production had a pre–Broadway run at the Eisenhower Theatre in Washington D.C., 31 July–14 Sept.)

3. CRITICAL STUDIES

Normand Berlin   'Staring Directly at Man's Existence'   (1982)

. . . Always the 'literary' O'Neill as well as the nostalgic O'Neill, in *The Iceman Cometh* he draws not only from memory but also from Gorky's *The Lower Depths* and Ibsen's *The Wild Duck* and the Bible and Nietzsche and Strindberg. The last is especially felt in Hickey's confession, where the horror of marriage takes on a Strindbergian emphasis, but Strindberg also hovers over the marital agonies of Harry Hope and Jimmy Tomorrow. O'Neill's abiding interest in Greek drama surely inspired him to make the denizens of Hope's saloon a 'chorus' (the word itself mentioned a number of times in the stage directions), serving similar functions to the Greek chorus, especially in their utterances during Hickey's confession. Perhaps Greek drama prodded O'Neill to observe the unities in *The Iceman Cometh* and in all his last plays. Certainly the device is perfect for a dramatist who wishes to lock his characters in the present while they talk of the past which produced that present, a dramatist who wishes to achieve an intensity of emotional effect. And perhaps a specific Greek tragedy, Sophocles' *Oedipus Rex*, gave O'Neill the idea of having a murder buried in the past revealed in stages, as is Hickey's murder of Evelyn, thereby building up suspense as the audience waits for the next revelation. (In this technique, Ibsen may have been as strong an influence.)

The Iceman Cometh, as a result of what was happening in the world and what was happening to O'Neill personally, contains a dark view of man's condition, and is a startling contrast to the play written just before the twelve-year silence, *Days Without End* (1934). No religious affirmations here, no faith in God, just the need of men to carry on as best they can with the help of illusion and alcohol *and* the willingness of men to uphold the dreams of others. The latter points to the play's positive qualities, the understanding compassion that the play evokes. Here . . . a comparison with Beckett's *Waiting for Godot* seems apt, for the derelicts, like Didi and Gogo, frozen to their places and to the present time, looking forward to a tomorrow that never comes, do have each other and do endure. *The Iceman Cometh* seems to depart philosophically from the plays that O'Neill wrote previously, but this is not altogether true. Forces continue to work 'behind life' to control men's lives, the past controls the present and future, frustration remains the condition of man, there is darkness behind the door, life seems a dirty trick, 'hopeless hope' and alcohol remain important means for survival, the themes of love and death continue to dominate. But O'Neill's emphasis seems different, and his existential view of life seems more clear and more true, with O'Neill's method sharpening his meaning. The classical unities, the large cast of characters (offering a wide variety of dialects), the musical orchestration of words and effects, the graceful melding of the realistic and symbolic, the crude and the biblical, the four and one-half hours' playing time, the atmosphere of stagnation, the comedy-tragedy combination – all give *The Iceman Cometh* a density of texture and a truth to life that places it in a class by itself, different from O'Neill's preceding plays (although containing many similar themes and devices) and different from the plays that served as its models. In it O'Neill, like the Larry Slade of the play's last moments, seems to be staring directly at man's *existence*; perhaps only Shakespeare and Sophocles before him, and Beckett after him, have stared at it so unblinkingly.[1] A stunning accomplishment. . . .

SOURCE: extract from ch. 7 ('Endings') in *Eugene O'Neill* – 'Macmillan Modern Dramatists' series (London & Basingstoke, 1982), pp. 140–2.

NOTE

1. Two perceptive discussions of O'Neill's existential view in the play are: Robert Brustein's essay on it in J. H. Raleigh (ed.), *The Iceman Cometh: A Collection of Critical Essays* (Englewood Cliffs, N.J., 1968), pp. 92–102; and J. Dennis Rich, 'Exile Without Remedy: The Late Plays of Eugene O'Neill', in Virginia Floyd (ed.), *Eugene O'Neill: A World View* (New York, 1979), pp. 257–76.

St John Ervine   Counsels of Despair   (1948)

Mark Twain, when he was told that the Pilgrim Fathers had landed on Plymouth Rock, fervently wished that Plymouth Rock had landed on the Pilgrim Fathers. The wine of veneration for these pioneering puritans was even then turning to vinegar, and now there is not a newly naturalised immigrant from the slums of Europe who will do them reverence or refrain from thumbing his nose at them. Yet it was they who made America safe for Mr Ben Hecht. What a paradox it is that America, where energetic enterprise and undauntable individuality are more highly esteemed than elsewhere, should deride the Pilgrim Fathers and applaud, as its greatest playwright, Mr Eugene O'Neill, whose whole belief about life contradicts his country's! All his plays are contemptuous of people and denunciatory of human existence: a commination service without a hymn. He has no zest for life: it disgusts him; and he may be described as the last of the Cathari, that singular sect of [medieval] Christians who loathed life, refused fertility, in principle if not in practice, and gave their greatest admiration to suicide. Larry Slade, in his latest play, *The Iceman Cometh*, is a typical *credens* Cathar: one who professes, but does not practise, the faith in its extreme form. He has no will to live, nor any will to die; and he drifts down to Harry Hope's squalid bar to become one of its dreariest inhabitants: a dismal drunkard who has not the courage of his futile convictions, and can commit suicide only by deputy.

Mr O'Neill is as puritanical as Mr Shaw, but his puritanism, unlike Mr Shaw's, unlike Milton's, unlike Andrew Marvell's, has no grace or geniality. It is sour stuff, and makes a Pilgrim Father, in comparison with Mr O'Neill, seem a blood relation of Sir Toby Belch. Yet no one denounces puritans so frequently and so ferociously as Mr O'Neill, who spits and spews upon their tombs as if they had done him personal injury. A man has only to mention that he is a Methodist minister to receive the entire contents of Mr O'Neill's vast vials of wrath. The Rev. Hutchins Light, in an incoherent piece, *Dynamo*, catches it severely; and a minister's son, Theodore Hickman, the protagonist of *The Iceman Cometh*, rails against his father as if he were the original owner of horns and hooves. His fury against puritans is so fierce that it appears to be pathological. Hickman, who has been created in the fallacy, refuted by fact, that the children of the clergy generally go to the devil, tells the dreary sots in Hope's bar that his home was 'like a jail'. If it was, we may well believe that he made it one.

The puritanical Milton was not the first of our poets to say

> The mind is its own place, and in itself
> Can make a Heav'n of Hell, a Hell of Heav'n
> *P. Lost*, ii 254–5

That roistering Elizabethan, Marlowe, slain in such a 'dive' as

Harry Hope's, was equally certain that each of us makes his own hell. Mephistophilis, when Faustus inquires where hell is, replies:

> ... where we are is hell,
> And where hell is, there must we ever be: ...

Mr O'Neill's drunken 'drummer', accusing his father of his own fault, describes a home which in no way, save that of being a minister's, resembles the one so lovingly portrayed by Thomas Lamont in his charming reminiscences, *A Boyhood in a Parsonage*, nor is his description reconcilable with the extraordinary number of great men and women, in America and Great Britain, who were born in rectories and manses. Mr F. C. S. Lowell, in *Munsey's Magazine* for September 1907, shows that 'nearly one in 12 of the Americans who have risen to distinction are clergyman's sons'. They include Emerson and Oliver Wendell Holmes.

Our own list is not negligible. It contains Addison, Matthew Arnold, Jane Austen, F. H. Bradley, the Brontës, John Buchan, Coleridge, Cowper, Crashaw, Cudworth, Drake, Froude, Mrs Gaskell, Goldsmith, J. R. Green, T. H. Green, Hallam, Warren Hastings, Hobbes, Hazlitt, Jenner, Keble, Charles Kingsley, Marvell, Nelson, Sir Joshua Reynolds, Cecil Rhodes, Henry Sidgwick, Tennyson, the Wesleys, Sir David Wilkie, Wolfe, Sir Christopher Wren and several hundred others. This nation would be greatly reduced in mental status if our rectories and manses had been barren. Students of the drama who are constrained by earnest teachers in co-educational schools to pore upon the works of Mr O'Neill as if they were the Holy Writ might well wonder how he, the son of devout Irish Roman Catholics, and brought up in a well-found theatrical family, knows anything about clerical homes, where means are usually small, and can assert with so much violent emphasis that they are sinks of iniquity where children are certain to be damned. Hickman is the only minister's child who frequents Hope's bar. What damned the rest of them to that? We can recall only one man with a load of clerical ancestors, and on both sides too, whose prospects of salvation have been hopelessly, if willingly, compromised: Karl Marx.

The question is not idly raised. It is strictly germane to Mr O'Neill's philosophy, if, indeed, philosophy is a word which is applicable to the mass of indisciplined emotions and jejune opinions which appear in his plays. This Cathar differs from his predecessors, from Manichee to Tolstoy and Ruskin, in a fundamental respect. They despaired of this life; he despairs of any. All other Cathari, Manicheans, Albigensians and what not,[1] loathed human life because they had a profound faith in a better one, and counted time spent here as wasted. The wise Cathar was one who quickly rid himself of humanity so that he might enjoy eternal felicity. But Mr O'Neill, the neo-Cathar, has no hope of anything better, here or hereafter. The world is futile and so are its inhabitants. There is no other world, and this one had better be ended. Let us therefore drink ourselves to death if we have not enough courage to blow out our brains. The people who frequent Harry Hope's bar are of different nationalities: American, Afrikaaner, English, German, Irish, Italian, Scottish and Negro; but they are all sots and spongers. The only workers among them are the barmen, who are pimps. The three women are prostitutes. That, according to Mr O'Neill, is mankind. There is nothing here of courage and endurance, nothing of unflinching faith, nothing of self-sacrifice deliberately made. The O'Neill world is a dirty pub, frequented by drunks and disorderlies and shiftless loafers; and periodically raided by corrupt cops.

Into this assembly of despair comes Hickman, the breezy boozer, who visits the bar occasionally for an orgy. But he is now a changed man: he has acquired a belief, and after the fashion of converts, is eager to proselytise. They must all do what he has done, confront fact, and acknowledge themselves to be what they are. If the pimp will admit that he is a pimp, if the prostitute will confess her occupation, if the sot and sponger will own up . . . then their misery will end. They undergo against their will some sort of conversion, but their regeneration renders them more futile than before; and when they learn that Hickman has solved his problem by murdering his wife, they relapse with relief. The swine return to their swill. They are, Slade asserts, converts to death.

The Iceman Cometh is not a brief decline into despair by an idealist who loses heart when he compares people as they are with people as he wishes them to be. Mr O'Neill is not Shakespeare writing *Timon of Athens*, with *The Tempest* still in his head. The Mr O'Neill who wrote *Beyond the Horizon* in 1920 is the Mr O'Neill [whose] *The Iceman Cometh* [was performed] in 1946; and we must take him with some seriousness, since his countrymen applaud him loudly, calling him their greatest playwright and placing him in august company. He has received the Pulitzer Prize three times. He was awarded the Nobel Prize in 1936, when he was forty-eight; a prize which has been capriciously awarded since 1914. Mr Shaw had to wait for it until he was sixty-nine. It was withheld from Thomas Hardy and H. G. Wells, but given to Mr Sinclair Lewis and Mrs Pearl Buck. Mr O'Neill's work has now been published and performed in many countries, although it has been less warmly received in Europe, and especially in France, than it has been in America. He is entitled, therefore, to be judged by the highest standards; and since *The Iceman Cometh*, the twenty-ninth of his plays to appear in Great Britain, seems to sum up his beliefs, its publication justifies us in attempting to estimate his rank. Is he, as many of his countrymen assert, of the same stature as Aeschylus and Shakespeare? He himself has not disclaimed the comparison. He has, indeed, insisted on it by using themes they used.

The most obvious difference between Aeschylus, Shakespeare and Mr O'Neill is that the two former loved mankind, but the last feels only contemptuous pity for it. The strongest passion animating his character is hate. A Desert Father was not more disdainful of existence than Mr O'Neill, who finds nothing inspiring in the sight of Caliban looking up to the beautiful Miranda. There is no sign of nobility in the characters who populate his plays. Not one of them has been made in the image of God. All of them bear the mark of the beast. The best of them are only negatively good, inertly abstaining from evil as if they were less in love with virtue than terrified of vice. Wandering through his underworld, and holding our noses as we wander, we have difficulty in believing that even it could have existed without one positively good and likable inhabitant. Nobel, in his will, laid down a law to guide adjudicators in awarding his Prize for Literature. It should be given 'to the person who shall have produced in the fields of literature the most distinguished work of an idealistic tendency'. The word *idealistic* is susceptible of various interpretations. It can be made applicable to Swift, even when he is writing about the Houyhnhms, but one must stretch and strain it severely to find its applicability to Mr O'Neill, whose world is a bestiary full of vulpine animals and crushed worms.

His characters are ineffectual egotists, whining for opportunities they are incapable of using. The most virile of them, the sailors and stokers in the early sea-plays, are mindless creatures, clawing and clutching like dying dinosaurs; and those who show some signs of contact with intelligence are impotent. In spite of the difference in their colour and physique. Yank in *The Hairy Ape*, and Robert Mayo in *Beyond the Horizon*, and the Negro student, Jim Harris, in *All God's Chillun Got Wings*, are closely akin; equally inept and empty. The leading characters in such plays as *The First Man, Welded, The Great God Brown* and *Days Without End*, who may be called 'intellectuals', are embarrassingly puerile, causing us to wonder how they managed to keep out of asylums. Marco Polo in *Marco Millions*, and Juan Ponce de Leon in *The Fountain*, are fustian figures, as futile and dispiriting as Emma Crosby in *Diff'rent*. Man, Mr O'Neill invites us to believe, is a puny creature who vainly dreams of high achievements, but is dogged by disaster. The desponding Gael has overpowered Mr O'Neill; and where there might have been poetic acclamation, there is only shrill and petulant complaint. It was Mommsen who said 'the Celts have shaken all states and have founded none'.[2] Mr O'Neill, in his despondent drama of despair, seems eager and ambitious to prove him right.

'Of the thirty-seven O'Neill plays I have seen or read', Mr Barrett Clark remarks in a hasty survey of them, 'there are only five in which there is no murder, death, suicide or insanity. In the others, I find a total of eight suicides and one unsuccessful attempt, twelve important murders (not counting incidental episodes); twenty-six deaths, nearly all due to violence; and eight cases of insanity.' Mr Clark's calculation was made in 1933. His figures can now be increased. Preoccupation with violence, however, is not Mr O'Neill's prime fault. An estimate of violent deaths in Shakespeare would make the Newgate Calendar seem pure as undriven snow. At the end of *Hamlet*, the stage is strewn with dead bodies, all of them violently done to death. Eight persons in that play are murdered. The heroine goes out of her mind and is drowned. Even Mr O'Neill has not indulged in so much slaughter in a single work. His supreme defect is his morbidity and febrile despair, his pathological contempt for people. Mr Somerset Maugham is not so disdainful of mortal motives as Mr O'Neill; is, indeed, less cruelly, because he is more cynically, contemptuous of them. There is greater pity for people in Mr Maugham than in Mr O'Neill, but neither of them seems to have noticed man's nobility, or to have observed his incessant efforts to rise to finer conditions, or to feel the slightest admiration for his courage under adversity. Mr O'Neill, indeed, has a perverse and sadistic desire to invert the nobility other men have seen. Shakespeare shows us a Caliban lifting up his eyes from the slime in which he flounders to gaze on loveliness and grace, but Mr O'Neill, in *The Hairy Ape*, finds his Caliban no more than a vicious gorilla, disguised as a man, who is infuriated by the fear and contempt he inspires in a multi-millionaire's degenerate daughter. His Miranda never meets a Ferdinand who makes her exclaim:

> O wonder!
> How many goodly creatures are there   here!
> How beauteous mankind is! O brave new world,
> That has such people in it.   [*Tempest*, V i 181–4]

She is, her aunt declares, 'a natural born ghoul', whose dilettante slumming is an excuse for indulging her morbid craving for sensation.

When she sees Yank, the hairy ape, she faints with horror, murmuring, 'Oh, the filthy beast'! Yank, enraged by her disgust, swears to revenge himself, but he never sees her again, nor does she re-enter the play, where she appears only in two short scenes. Her insignificance is a cardinal defect in it. The hairy ape begins a futile war on society. But his end is casual. He visits the monkey-house of New York Zoo, where he sees a gorilla, and enters its cage, and is crushed to death in its arms. The gorilla then escapes to ravage! . . . Here, as always, Mr O'Neill is surprisingly insufficient. Shakespeare superbly surpasses him in *The Tempest*. There is more in H. G. Wells's *Food of the Gods*.

The Hairy Ape is not the only play in which Mr O'Neill challenges comparison with Shakespeare. His work on miscegenation, *All God's Chillun Got Wings*, ought to be better than *Othello*, since its subject is more familiar to any American than it could have been to any Elizabethan; but in this play, too, Mr O'Neill comes a terrible cropper, bringing no thought to his theme. His Negro has no magnitude. Othello is a great soldier; Desdemona has a proud spirit, even when she is most submissive, and her nature is noble. But there is neither pride nor nobility in the slum drab, Ella Downey, who marries Jim Harris, the Negro who yearns to be a lawyer when he has only the mental equipment of a Pullman Car attendant. Ella does not marry Jim, as Desdemona married the Moor, because her heart is stirred to admiration of his great and heroic deeds. She marries him in neurotic despair, after a spell in the stews. Robert Mayo, in *Beyond the Horizon*, is a peevish Hamlet who whines and snivels through his futile and dismal life. This play is intellectually, as well as physically, tuberculous. Its lungs are full of holes. Mr O'Neill does not let his audience off a single hacking cough. One reference to Julius Caesar's epilepsy – 'he hath the falling sickness' – suffices for Shakespeare, but if Mr O'Neill had written the play, the emperor would have thrown innumerable fits through fifteen garrulous acts. It is in this play, *Beyond the Horizon*, the first of his long works to be performed, that the theme of all Mr O'Neill's plays is set out: frustration and disillusionment. Robert Mayo is the progenitor of a long line of ineffectual egotists whose ambition far exceeds their ability. Incapable of anything but sentimental longing for what he can neither attain nor do, he groans against life, floundering from folly to folly, and blaming existence for his inefficiency. In a burst of flatulent oratory, he tells his broken-spirited wife, herself little better than he is, that he will sell the farm he has inherited and start a new life in a city. 'I'll write – or something!' He has never shown the slightest sign of ability to write even a handbill. The remark is typical of his general impotence. 'I'll write – or something!' He is a crapulous Micawber whose wife is rightly eager to desert him. . . .

[Ervine's discussion here of *Mourning Becomes Electra* is transferred, as a distinct item, to section 3 of Part One, above – Ed.]

Mr O'Neill's technique has been extolled for its experimental character, but it is clumsy and sometimes surprisingly ingenuous. He was not a novice when he wrote *Beyond the Horizon*, yet that play, which has six scenes when three would suffice, is singularly incontinent and full of loose ends. One of the characters is a two-year-old child with a substantial speaking part! . . . A farmer brings a team of plough horses into the first scene for two minutes. Neither he nor they serve any purpose. In Act Two, scene 1, Robert tells his wife, Ruth, to prepare herself for bad news, but is interrupted before he can break it to her. The news is never imparted. The soliloquies could not be removed from *Hamlet* without leaving a bleeding wound, but there would not be a scar if almost the whole of the soliloquies were removed from *Strange Interlude*, a play which would be greatly improved if the last three scenes were omitted. Years leap from decade to decade in Mr O'Neill's work in a very careless rapture. We need not become slaves to the doctrine of dramatic unities alleged to have been laid down by Aristotle, who was not a dramatist, to find fault with this scattering of time. To keep a play 'as far as possible within a single circuit of the sun, or something near that', is a good general rule, but if it were made into a law which must not be broken, an attempt which Aristotle did not make, neither *A Winter's Tale* nor *Back to Methuselah* could have been written.

To defy the alleged Aristotelian law, however, is one thing and to treat time as confetti is another. Thirty years separate the two acts of *Diff'rent*, a play which ends with incredible suicides. Fifteen years divide the first and second scenes of *Marco Millions*. There are eleven years between the sixth and seventh acts of *Strange Interlude*. The first part of *The Fountain* is separated from the second by twenty years. Manifestly, Mr O'Neill's people did not cease to exist during these long intervals. Things must have happened to them. Their characters must have developed. But experience and growth are not revealed, and the intervals are arbitrary. There are tricks with stage directions in almost every play Mr O'Neill has written, many of them naively pretentious, as in *The Hairy Ape*, where we are informed five or six times that the stokers, when they speak in chorus, have 'a brazen, metallic quality as if their throats were phonograph horns'. Each chorused ejaculation 'is followed by a chorus of hard, barking laughter'. This is the sort of stuff that might be written by an earnest sophomore who has listened too long to professors of dramatic literature at chatauquas in the Rocky Mountains. There is indeed an air of juvenility about most of Mr O'Neill's work. An adolescent who had just heard the facts of life, and felt very indignant about them, might have written *The First Man*. He is terribly verbose, making Mr Shaw seem tongue-tied. *The Iceman Cometh* is at least an hour too long. There are no memorable words in his dialogue, not a single sentence which is likely to become part of his country's speech or to remain in any man's recollection as an illuminating phrase. Some of his subhuman characters, such as the Cabots in *Desire Under the Elms*, are accustomed to murmur 'purty' when they see a sunset, but that is as far as any of them gets in the search for beauty. The Irish stoker, Mick Burke, in *Anna Christie*, must have spent hours in learning Synge's plays by heart. He talks as we might have expected [Synge's] Christy Mahon to talk after he had joined the IRA. This is one of the best of the O'Neill plays, but it is marred by melodrama and rendered ludicrous at the end by Mick's dismay when he thinks that Anna, whom he is about to marry, may be a Protestant!*

But there is a sense of the theatre in the plays which proves that the hours spent by Mr O'Neill in listening to his father acting in *Monte Cristo* were not spent without effect. How skilfully he can construct a play, how charmingly he can create presentable people is apparent . . . in *Ah, Wilderness!*; a comedy on which one comes with mingled pleasure and surprise. How much of Mr O'Neill's popularity in America depends upon his extensive use of gutter speech and low-grade characters is hard to say. *The Iceman Cometh* is entirely inhabited by such people, uttering very vigorously the language of the stews. Even in *Ah Wilderness!* there is a scene full of it.

There was a fog on the night in 1916 when Mr O'Neill's first play to be publicly performed, a short sea-piece entitled *Bound East for Cardiff*, was produced in a fish-shed on a wharf in Provincetown, on the coast of Massachusetts. The fish-shed had been transfigured, and was now The Wharf Theatre, with a 'capacity' of ninety persons: a little smaller than the bandbox in Bergen in which Bjornson and Ibsen learnt their craft. The cast included the author, who, however, failed to convince his audience that his father lived again on the stage. The salt tide seeped through holes in the floor as the band of unsophisticated Greenwich villagers – who had fled from the disenchantments of New York to settle on that bleak and solitary coast, to regenerate the drama and enrich the minds of artless

* [Ed. Mick Burke is Ervine's error for Mat Burke.]

fishermen with news of *Das Kapital* – watched the birthpangs of America's greatest dramatist. The fog entered Mr O'Neill's soul that night and has remained there ever since. 'Fog, fog, fog, all bloody time', cries Anna Christie's Swedish-American father as he shakes his fist at the universe. 'You can't see where you vas going, no!' And Anna herself, an embittered drab, sums us up. 'We're all poor nuts', she moans. The fog has thickened in *The Iceman Cometh*; a thick, yellow, suffocating fog; and it makes Larry Slade, the spineless Celt, a convert to death, too cowardly to seek the end he craves. When Faustus, in Marlowe's play, summoned Alexander the Great and Helen of Troy from the grave, they came, but did not speak. Like Bottom, they had been translated, and the mind of man could not conceive what they had seen. But when Mr O'Neill, in *Lazarus* [sc. *Laughed* – Ed.], summons the brother of Martha and Mary from the tomb, Lazarus comes in a fit of the giggles. Even the giggles have ceased for Larry Slade. There is nothing left for him but a delusive bottle and the hope that he will one day die of delirium tremens.

SOURCE: unsigned article ('Counsels of Despair') in the *Times Literary Supplement* (10 April 1948).

NOTES

1. [Ed.] *Manicheans*: believers in the dualistic cosmogony of the Persian mystic, Mani (c. 216–76 AD) who postulated an eternal conflict between Basic Good and Basic Evil, Light and Darkness, in a universe devoid of any superior regulating Power save, in some measure, the transient 'balance' achieved at a given time between these warring forces. *Albigensians*: a religious community, originally centred on Albi in southern France in the twelfth century, fiercely suppressed (but not extirpated) by papal-sanctioned local 'crusades', 1209–29. The sects' beliefs were strongly influenced by Manicheanism and the Catharist doctrine of extreme asceticism.

2. [Ed.] Theodore Mommsen (1817–1903): German historian and classicist, author of the great *History of Rome* (pro-Caesarist in political tendency) which, with his editorship of the massive *Corpus Inscriptionum Latimarum*, made him a paladin of world-revered German scholarship of the nineteenth century. His influence on the development of German cultural and political state-nationalism was very great.

Brooks Atkinson   Feuding Again   (1948)

After an uneasy armed truce, while more desperate issues were being fought over, the battle of the London and New York critics is resuming. The *Literary Supplement* of *The Times* of London has gone to some scholarly pains to prove that Eugene O'Neill is humbug and that his eminence is the 'pipe-dream' of American adolescents and chauvinists. If the crackpot Thomas committee in Washington is looking for some hot evidence of un-American activities, it could make good use of this jeremiad in the *Times Literary Supplement*. The writer denounces O'Neill for holding beliefs that contradict those of correct Americans and for not following the teachings of the Pilgrim Fathers, who came from England – although somewhat rebelliously if I remember correctly.

Even for a critic the animadversions of the *Literary Supplement* writer are excessively obtuse and prejudiced. Since H. G. Wells and Thomas Hardy never received the Nobel Prize, he thinks that the award to O'Neill was unworthy. He chides O'Neill for not obeying Aristotle's rules more dutifully. He says that O'Neill is not equal to Shakespeare or Aeschylus, and is inferior to Somerset Maugham – although Maugham, he suggests, is not exactly above reproach. O'Neill's verbosity, says the *Literary Supplement*'s writer, makes Shaw seem tongue-tied by comparison. Discussing *The Hairy Ape* – one of the bluntest and most powerful plays in the language (even Somerset Maugham seems supercilious by comparison) – he says: 'This is the sort of stuff that might be written by an earnest sophomore who has listened too long to professors of dramatic literature at chautauquas in the Rocky Mountains.' Yes, that's what he says; it's there in plain print on fairly good paper.

But the most entertaining of his objurgations is his lengthy and pious treatise on O'Neill's cavalier treatment of a clergyman's son in *The Iceman Cometh*. Hickey, the mad 'drummer', is a minister's son and does not look back with joy on his youth. According to *The Times* writer, this shows how misguided O'Neill is. Quoting F. C. S. Lowell in *Munsey's Magazine* of September 1907 (there's research for you!), *The Times* writer points out that nearly one in twelve of America's men of distinction were clergymen's sons. He mentions thirty-four celebrated English people who were clergymen's children – which is most reassuring – and wonders how O'Neill 'can assert with so much violence that [clerical homes] are sins of iniquity where children are certain to be damned'. To the best of my knowledge, O'Neill has never made any such general assumptions; he is not that foolish. Only a pedant hopelessly raddled with prejudice would ever turn up with anything so irrelevant to the subject of O'Neill's quality as a dramatist.

If the Cato of the *Literary Supplement* does not like O'Neill, there is no point in trying to convince him that he does. Many Americans do not like him at all. And even his best friends do not conceive of him as perfect. As a prose stylist he has always been curiously inadequate. He cannot wrap his singing robes around him, like Milton. The recent Fordham production of *Lazarus Laughed* painfully disclosed the poverty of his use of words when he is trying to express ecstasy or exaltation. Nor is O'Neill a thinker. Although he is always digging at the roots of life, his intellectual conclusions are hardly impressive. Under the impression that he is being profound, he habitually overwrites because he cannot prove a point except by repeating it over and over. As a conscious artist, O'Neill lacks grace.

But these are superficial things. Although they are valued highly by people satisfied with manners, they are not conclusive. For the genius of O'Neill is the raw boldness and the elemental strength of his attack upon outworn concepts of destiny. Don't be misled by the crudeness of his characters and the gutter argot they speak. For he, too, is a moral writer. He thinks the spiritual glories of America have been sold out for materialistic gains, which is a moral idea. He thinks that modern civilisation is godless and that it has not found a substitute for God – and that, too, is a moral idea.

Like Chekhov, he thinks that civilisation is sick. Although Chekhov composed rueful portraits of the sickness, O'Neill, whose emotions are more powerful, has been feverishly probing into the disease. He is not revelling in gloom and corruption; to him those are symptoms of something more horrible and fatal. Although this may be unpleasant, only a very smug man would dare assert that there is not a lot of truth in it. On the evidence of the pious disdain of the *Literary Supplement* article, I would prefer to trust the savage vitality of O'Neill's work, for I feel more secure in the company of artists who are alive.

Under the spell of this tragic compulsion, O'Neill has written a number of silly plays, as he is the first to admit. But he came into our theatre at a time when most plays were aimless, post-prandial charades. A pioneer in method, he broke a number of the old moulds, shook up the drama as well as audiences and helped to transform the theatre into an art seriously related to life. In his most creative moments he has written the incomparable 'S. S. Glencairn' series,* *The Hairy Ape, Anna Christie, Desire Under the Elms* – which is a masterpiece of materialistic tragedy – *Marco Millions* (a scornful satire in the form of a masque), *Strange Interlude* and *Mourning Becomes*

* [Ed.] The 'S. S. Glencairn' series (named after the ship at the centre of the dramatic action) comprises *Bound East for Cardiff* (1916), *The Long Voyage Home* (1917), *In the Zone* (1917) and *The Moon of the Caribbees* (1918). The dates are the years of first production.

Electra – which is another masterpiece on a loftier plane. *Ah, Wilderness!* is a charming comedy of recollection, pleasing in style, though hardly equal to the main body of O'Neill's work.

Criticism is a minor category of literature and the requirements for it, fortunately, are not high. But even in this field a writer ought to be able to know something about life and recognise vitality where it exists. The peevish article in the *Times Literary Supplement* overlooks the one thing in O'Neill that is inescapable: the passionate depth and vitality of his convictions. Nothing said about him is worth the paper it is printed on unless it recognises the vitality he has brought into the theatre. Nobody is so impervious to vitality as a writer who has none.

SOURCE: article ("Feuding Again') in the *New York Times* (25 April 1948).

Eric Bentley   Trying to Like O'Neill   (1952)

It would be nice to like O'Neill. He is the leading American playwright; damn him, damn all; and damning all is a big responsibility. It is tempting to damn the rest and make of O'Neill an exception. He *is* an exception in so many ways. He has cared less for temporary publicity than for lasting and deserved fame. When he was successful on Broadway he was not sucked in by Broadway. The others have vanity; O'Neill has self-respect. No dickering with the play-doctors in Manhattan hotel rooms. He had the guts to go away and the guts to stay away. O'Neill has always had the grown-up writer's concern for that continuity and development which must take place quietly and from within. In a theatre that chiefly attracts idiots and crooks, he was a model of good sense and honor.

In 1946 he was raised to the American peerage: his picture was on the cover of *Time*. The national playwright was interviewed by the nationalist press. It was his chance to talk rot and be liked for it. It was his chance to spout optimistic uplift and play the patriotic pundit. But O'Neill said:

I'm going on the theory that the United States, instead of being the most successful country in the world is the greatest failure . . . because it was given everything more than any other country. Through moving as rapidly as it has, it hasn't acquired any real roots. Its main idea is that everlasting game of trying to possess your own soul by the possession of something outside it too. . . .

Henry Luce possesses a good many things besides his own soul. He possesses *Life* as well as *Time*, and in the former he published an editorial complaining of the lack of inspiration to be found in the national playwright. In *The Iceman Cometh* there were no princes and heroes, only bums and drunks. This was 'democratic snobbism'. Henry Luce was evidently in favor of something more aristocratic (the pin-up girls in his magazine notwithstanding). Inevitably, though, what the aristocrats of *Time Inc.* objected to in O'Neill was his greatest virtue: his ability to stay close to the humbler forms of American life as he had seen them. It is natural that his claim to be a national playwright should rest chiefly on a critical and realistic attitude to American life which they reject. Like the three great Irish playwrights, O'Neill felt his 'belonging' to his country so deeply that he took its errors to heart; and though admittedly he wished his plays to be universal, they all start at home; they are specifically a criticism of American life. *Marco Millions* is only the bluntest of his critical studies. Interest in the specifically American pattern of living sustains his lightest work, *Ah, Wilderness!* New England patterns are integral to *Desire under the Elms* and *Mourning Becomes Electra*, the latter being an attempt at an *Oresteia* in terms of American history, with the Civil War as an equivalent of the Trojan War. The protagonist of *The Iceman Cometh* is a product of Hoosier piety, a study much more deeply rooted in American life than Arthur Miller's of a salesman going to his death. It would be nice to like O'Neill because the Luce magazines *dis*like him – that is, because he is opposed to everything they stand for.

Last autumn, when I was invited to direct the German-language *première* of *The Iceman* [in Zürich], along with Kurt Hirschfeld, I decided I should actually succeed in liking O'Neill. I reminded myself that he had been honored with prefaces by Joseph Wood Krutch and Lionel Trilling, that he had aroused enthusiasm in the two hardest-to-please of the New York critics, Stark Young and George Jean Nathan, and so forth. I even had a personal motive to aid and abet the pressure of pure reason. My own published strictures on O'Neill had always been taken as a display of gratuitous pugnacity, amusing or reprehensible according to my reader's viewpoint. Now, it is a fallacy that drama critics are strongly attached to their own opinions; actually they would far rather be congratulated on having the flexibility to change their minds. Under a rain of dissent one begins to doubt one's opinions and to long for the joy that is not confined to heaven when a sinner repenteth. In short, I should have been glad to write something in praise of O'Neill, and I actually did lecture – and speak on the Swiss radio –

as an O'Neillite. If this seems disingenuous, I can only plead that I spoke as a director, not as critic, and that it is sometimes a great relief to do so. There is something too godlike about criticism; it is a defiance of the injunction to men: 'Judge not, that ye be not judged'; it is a strain. And if it would be subhuman to give up the critical attitude for mere liking and disliking the directorial, interpretative attitude seems a more mature and challenging alternative.

Both critic and director are aware of faults, but whereas it is the critic's job to point them out, it is the director's job to cover them up, if only by strongly bringing out a play's merits. It is not true that a director accepts a play with its faults on its head, that he must follow the playwright even into what he believes to be error. He cannot be a self-respecting interpreter without following his own taste and judgement. Thus, Hirschfeld and I thought we were doing our best by O'Neill in toning certain things down and playing others full blast. Specifically, there seemed to us to be in *The Iceman Cometh* a genuine and a non-genuine element, the former, which we regarded as the core, being realistic, the latter, which we took as inessential excrescence, being expressionistic. I had seen what came of author-worshipping direction in the Theatre Guild production, where all O'Neill's faults were presented to the public with careful reverence. In order to find the essential – or at least the better – O'Neill we agreed to forgo much O'Neillism.

Our designer, Teo Otto, agreed. I told him of Robert Edmond Jones's Rembrandtesque lighting and of the way in which Jones, in his sketches, tried to create the phantasmagoria of a Strindberg dream play; but Otto, though we discussed various sensational ways of setting the play – with slanting floors and Caligari corridors or what not – agreed in the end that we would be taking O'Neill's story more seriously if we tried simply to underline the sheer reality, the sheer banality and ugliness, of its locale. Instead of darkness, and dim, soulfully colored lights, we used a harsh white glare, suggesting unshaded electric bulbs in a bare room. And the rooms *were* bare. On the walls Otto suggested the texture of disintegrating plaster: a dripping faucet was their only ornament. A naked girder closed the rooms in from above. And, that this real setting be seen as setting and not as reality itself, the stage was left open above the girder. While Hirschfeld and I were busy avoiding the abstractness of expressionism, Otto made sure that we did not go to the other extreme – a piddling and illusion-mongering naturalism.

To get at the core of reality in *The Iceman* – which is also its artistic, its dramatic core – you have to cut away the rotten fruit of unreality around it. More plainly stated: you have to cut. The play is far too long – not so much in asking that the audience sit there so many hours as on sheer internal grounds. The main story is meant to have suspense, but we are suspended so long we forget all about it. One can cut a good many of Larry's speeches since he is forever rephrasing a pessimism that is by no means hard to understand the first time. One can cut down the speeches of Hugo since they are both too long and too pretentious. It is such a pretentiousness, replete with obvious and unimaginative symbols, that constitutes the expressionism of the play. Hugo is a literary conception – by Gorky out of Dostoyevsky.

We cut about an hour out of the play. It wasn't always easy. Not wishing to cut out whole characters, we mutilated a few till they had, I'm afraid, no effective existence. But we did not forget that some of the incidental details of *The Iceman* are among O'Neill's finest achievements. Nothing emerged more triumphantly from our shortened, crisper version than the comic elements. With a dash of good humor O'Neill can do more than with all his grandiloquent lugubriousness. Nothing struck my fancy more, in our production, than the little comedy of the Boer general and the English captain. O'Neill is also very good at a kind of homely genre painting. Harry's birthday party with its cake and candles and the whores singing his late wife's favorite song, 'She Is the Sunshine of Paradise Alley', is extremely well done; and no other American playwright could do it without becoming either too sentimental or too sophisticated. We tried to build the scene up into a great theatric image, and were assisted by a magnificent character actor as Harry (Kurt Horwitz). It is no accident that the character of Harry came out so well both in New York and in Zürich: the fact is that O'Neill can draw such a man more pointedly than he can his higher-flying creations.

I am obviously a biased judge, but I think Zürich was offered a more dramatic evening than New York. The abridging of the text did lay bare the main story and release its suspense. We can see the action as presumably we were meant to see it. There is Hickey, and there is Parritt. Both are pouring out their false confessions and professions and holding back their essential secret. Yet, inexorably, though against their conscious will, both are seeking punishment. Their two stories are brought together through Larry Slade, whose destiny, in contrast to his intention, is to extract the secret of both protagonists. Hickey's secret explodes, and Larry at last gives Parritt what he wants: a death sentence. The upshot of the whole action is that Larry is brought from a posturing and oratorical pessimism to a real despair. Once the diffuse speeches are trimmed and the minor characters reduced to truly minor proportions, Larry is revealed as the centre of the play, and the audience can watch the two stories being played out before him.

A systematic underlining of all that is realistic in the play did, as we hoped it would, bring the locale – Jimmy the Priest's – to successful theatrical realisation, despite the loss of much of O'Neill's detail. It gave body and definition to what otherwise would have remained insubstantial and shapeless; the comedy was sharpened, the sentiment purified. I will not say that the production realised the idea of the play which Hirschfeld, Otto, and I entertained. In theatre there is always too much haste and bungling for that. One can only say that the actuality did not fall farther short of the idea in this instance than in others.

And yet it was not a greater success with the public than the New York production, and whereas some New York critics were restrained by awe before the national playwright, the Swiss critics, when they were bored, said so. My newly won liking for O'Neill would perhaps have been unshaken by the general opinion – except that in the end I couldn't help sharing it.

I enjoyed the rehearsal period – unreservedly. I didn't have to conceal my reservations about O'Neill out of tact. They ceased to exist. They were lost in the routine, the tension, and the delight of theatre work. I don't mean to suggest that you could lose yourself thus in any script, however bad; there are scripts that bear down on a director with all the dead weight of their fatuity. But in an O'Neill script there are problems, technical and intellectual, and every one a challenge. I gladly threw myself headlong into that mad joy of the theatre in which the world and its atomic bombs recede and one's own first night seems to be the goal toward which creation strives.

The shock of the first night was the greater. It was not one of those catastrophic first nights when on all faces you can see expectancy fading into ennui or lack of expectancy freezing into a smug I Told You So. But, theatrically speaking, mild approval is little better. Theatrical art is a form of aggression. Like the internal-combustion engine it proceeds by a series of explosions. Because it is in the strictest sense the most shocking of the arts, it has failed most utterly when no shock has been felt, and it has failed in a large measure when the shock is mild. *The Iceman* aroused mild interest, and I had to agree that *The Iceman* was only mildly interesting. When I read the critics, who said about my O'Neill production precisely what I as critic had said about other O'Neill productions, my period of liking O'Neill was over.

Of course there were shortcomings that O'Neill could not be blamed for. We were presenting him in German, and in addition to the normal translation problems there were two special ones: that of translating contrasting dialects and that of reproducing the tone of American, semi-gangster, hard-boiled talk. There was little the translator could do about the dialects. She wisely did not lay under contribution the various regions of Germany or suggest foreign accents, and her idea of using a good deal of Berlin slang had to be modified for our Swiss public. One simply forwent many of O'Neill's effects or tried to get them by non-verbal means – and by that token one realised how much O'Neill does in the original with the various forms of the vernacular (real or histrionic). One also realises how much he uses the peculiarly American institution of Tough Talk, now one of the conventions of the American stage: a lingo that the young playwright learns, just as at one time the young poet learned Milton's poetic diction. In German there seems to be no real equivalent of this lingo, because there is no equivalent of the psychology from which it springs and to which it caters. And there is no teaching the actors how to speak their lines in the hard-boiled manner. Irony is lost, and the dialogue loses its salt. This loss and that of dialect flavor were undoubtedly great deficiencies.

But not the greatest. I saw the production several times and, in addition to the flaws for which we of the Schauspielhaus were responsible, there stood out clearer each time the known, if not notorious, faults of O'Neill. True, he is a man of the theatre and, true, he is an eloquent writer composing, as his colleagues on Broadway usually do not, under the hard compulsion of something he has to say. But his gifts are mutually frustrating. His sense of theatrical form is frustrated by an eloquence that decays into mere repetitious garrulousness. His eloquence is frustrated by the extreme rigidity of the theatrical mould into which it is poured – jelly in an iron jar. Iron. Study, for example, the stage directions of *The Iceman*, and you will see how carefully O'Neill has drawn his ground plan. There everyone sits – a row of a dozen and a half men. And as they sit, the plot progresses; as each new stage is reached, the bell rings, and the curtain comes down. Jelly. Within the tyrannically, mechanically rigid scenes, there is an excessive amount of freedom. The order of speeches can be juggled without loss, and almost any speech can be cut in half.

The eloquence might of course be regarded as clothing that is necessary to cover a much too mechanical man. Certainly, though we gained more by abridging the play than we lost, the abridgment did call attention rather cruelly to the excessively schematic character of the play. Everything is contrived, *voulu*, drawn on the blackboard, thought out beforehand, imposed on the material by the dead hand of calculation. We had started out from the realisation that the most lifeless schemata in this over-schematic play are the expressionistic ones, but we had been too sanguine in hoping to conceal or cancel them. They are foreshadowed already in the table groupings of Act One (as specified in O'Neill's stage directions). They hold the last act in a death grip. Larry and Parritt are on one side shouting their duet. Hickey is in the centre singing his solo. And at the right, arranged en bloc, is everyone else, chanting their comments in what O'Neill himself calls a 'chorus'.

It would perhaps be churlish to press the point, were O'Neill's ambition in this last act not symptomatic both of his whole endeavor as a playwright and of the endeavor of many other serious playwrights in our time. It is the ambition to transcend realism. O'Neill spoke of it nearly thirty years ago in a program note on Strindberg:

It is only by means of some form of 'super-naturalism' that we may express in the theatre what we comprehend intuitively of that self-obsession which is the particular discount we moderns have to pay for the loan of life. The old naturalism – or realism if you will (I wish to God some genius were gigantic enough to define clearly the separateness of these terms once and for all!) – no longer applies. It represents our fathers' daring aspirations towards self-recognition by holding the family kodak up to ill-nature. But to us their audacity is blague, we have taken too many snapshots of each other in every graceless position. We have endured too much from the banality of surfaces.

So far, so good. This is a warning against that extreme and narrow form of realism generally known as naturalism. Everyone agrees. The mistake is to talk as if it followed that one must get away from realism altogether: a mistake repeated by every poetaster who thinks he can rise above Ibsen by writing flowerily (for example, Christopher Fry as quoted and endorsed by *Time*). Wherever O'Neill tries to clarify his non-realistic theory the only thing that is clear is lack of clarity. For example:

It was far from my idea in writing *The Great God Brown* that the background pattern of conflicting tides in the soul of man should ever overshadow and thus throw out of proportion the living drama of the recognizable human beings. ... I meant *it* always to be mystically within and behind them, giving them a significance beyond themselves, forcing itself through them to expression in mysterious words, symbols, actions they do not themselves comprehend. And that is as clearly as I wish an audience to comprehend *it*. *It* is Mystery – the mystery any one man or woman can feel but not understand as the meaning of any event – or accident – in any life on earth. And it is this mystery which I want to realize in the theatre.

I have italicised the word *it* to underline the shift in reference that takes place. The first two times 'it' is 'the background pattern of conflicting tides in the soul of man'. The third time 'it' is just a blur, meaning nothing in particular, exemplifying rather than clearing up the mystery that O'Neill finds important. An event can be mysterious, but how can its mystery be its meaning? And how can we know that its mystery is its meaning if we do 'not understand' it? And what would constitute a 'realisation' of such a phenomenon in the theatre?

In a letter to Arthur Hobson Quinn, O'Neill tries again. He has been seeking to be a poet, he says,

and to see the transfiguring nobility of tragedy, in as near the Greek sense as one can grasp it, in seemingly the most ignoble, debased lives. And just here is where I am most confirmed mystic too, for I'm always, always trying *to interpret Life in terms of lives, never just lives in terms of characters.* I'm always acutely conscious of the Force behind (Fate, God, our biological past creating our present, whatever one calls it – Mystery certainly) and of the one eternal tragedy of Man in his glorious, self-destructive struggle *to make the Force express him instead of being, as an animal is, an infinitesimal incident in its expression.* And my profound conviction is that this is the only subject worth writing about and that it is possible – or can be – to develop a tragic expression in terms of transfigured modern values and symbols in the theatre which may to some degree bring home to members of a modern audience their ennobling identity with the tragic figures on the stage. Of course, this is very much of a dream, but where theatre is concerned, one must have a dream and the Greek dream in tragedy is the noblest ever!

This time I have italicised phrases where we expect O'Neill to say something, where we even think for a moment that he *has* said something. Reading them several times over, we find that we could give them a meaning – but without any assurance that it is O'Neill's. What is interpreting 'Life in terms of lives' and what is 'mystical' about it? What does it mean to be 'expressed' by a Force – as against being an incident in 'its expression'? Isn't O'Neill comforting himself with verbiage? For what connection is there – beyond the external ones of *Mourning Becomes Electra* – between his kind of drama and the Greek? How could one be ennobled by identifying oneself with any of his characters?

It is no use wanting to get away from realism (or anything else) unless you know what you want to get away *to*. Raising a dust of symbols and poeticisms is not to give artistic expression to a sense of mystery. It is merely, in O'Neill's case, to take your eye off the object. (Cf. Ibsen: 'To be a poet is chiefly to see.') It seems to me that O'Neill's eye was off the object, and on Dramatic and Poetic Effects, when he composed the Hickey story. Not being clearly seen, the man is unclearly presented to the audience: O'Neill misleads them for several hours, then asks them to reach back into their memory and reinterpret all Hickey's actions and attitudes from the beginning. Is Hickey the character O'Neill needed as the man who tries to deprive the gang of their illusions? He (as it turns out) is a maniac. But if the attempt to disillude the gang is itself mad, it would have more dramatic point if made by a sane idealist (as in *The Wild Duck*).

Does O'Neill find the meaning of his story by looking at the people and the events themselves or by imposing it on them? There are ideas in the play, and we have the impression that what should be the real substance of it is mere (not always deft) contrivance to illustrate the ideas. The main ideas are two: first, the one we have touched on, that people may as well keep their illusions; second, that they should not hate and punish, but love and forgive. The whole structure of the play is so inorganic that it is hardly to be expected that the two ideas would be organically related. The difficulty is in finding what relation they do have. In a way the truth-illusion theme is a red herring, and, as in *Così è (se vi pare)* – *Right You Are* – the author's real interest is in the love-hate theme. Pirandello, however, presents the red herring *as* a red herring, relates his false theme to his real one. O'Neill is unclear because he fails to do so. A high official of the Theatre Guild remarked: 'The point is, you aren't *meant* to understand.' In Pirandello this is indeed the point of the Ponza/Frola story. Pirandello *makes* the point, and in art a point has to be made before it can be said to exist. For O'Neill it is merely a point he might have made. As things are, it is his play, and not life, that is unintelligible.

The Iceman, of course, has big intentions written all over it. Most of O'Neill's plays have big intentions written all over them. He has written of

the death of an old God and the failure of science and materialism to give any satisfying new one for the surviving primitive religious instinct to find a meaning for life in, and to comfort its fears of death with. It seems to me [he adds] anyone trying to do big work nowadays must have this subject behind all the little subjects of his plays or novels.

In other words, O'Neill's intentions as a writer are no less vast than Dostoyevsky's. *The Iceman* is his version of crime and punishment. What is surprising is not that his achievements fall below Dostoyevsky's but that critics – including some recent rehabilitators – have taken the will for the deed and find O'Neill's nobler 'conception' of theatre enough. 'Conception' is patently a euphemism for 'intention' and they are applauding O'Neill for strengthening the pavement of hell. In this they are not disingenuous; their own intentions are also good; they are simply a party to a general gullibility. People believe what they are told, and in our time a million units of human energy are spent on the telling to everyone rather than on examining what is told; reason is swamped by propaganda and publicity. Hence it is that an author's professions and intentions, broadcast not only by himself but by an army of interested and even disinterested parties, determine what people think his work is. The realm of false culture thus created is not all on one level; brows here, as elsewhere, may be high or low. No brows are higher indeed than those of the sub-intelligentsia. They spend their time seeking sublimities, works that provide the answers to the crying questions of our time, impassioned appeals for justice, daring indictments of tyranny, everything sure-fire. Seek and you shall find: a writer like O'Neill does not give them the optimism of an 'American century', but he provides profundities galore, and technical innovations, and (as he himself says) Mystery. Now, there is a large contingent of the subintelligentsia in the theatre world. They are seen daily at the Algonquin and nightly at Sardi's.[1] They don't all like O'Neill, yet his 'profound' art is inconceivable without them. O'Neill doesn't like *them*, but he needs them, and could never have dedicated himself to 'big work' had their voices not been in his ears telling him he was big. The man who could not be bribed by the Broadway tycoons was seduced by the Broadway intelligentsia.

At one time he performed a historic function, that of helping the American theatre to grow up. In all his plays an earnest attempt is made to interpret life; this fact in itself places O'Neill above his predecessors in American drama and beside his colleagues in the novel and in poetry. He was a good playwright in so far as he kept within the somewhat narrow range of his own sensibility. When he stays close to a fairly simple reality and when, by way of technique, he uses fairly simple forms of realism or fairly simple patterns of melodrama, he can render the bite and tang of reality or, alternatively, he can startle and stir us with his effects. If he is never quite a poet, he is occasionally able – as we have seen in *The Iceman* – to create the striking theatric image.

But the more he attempts, the less he achieves. . . .

SOURCE: extract from 'Trying to Like O'Neill', *Kenyon Review*, 14 (July 1952); reproduced as ch. 9 in Bentley's *In Search of Theater* (New York, 1955), pp. 220—31. (Continuation of Bentley's discussion, with particular regard to *Mourning Becomes Electra*, will be found in section 3 of Part One, above.)

NOTE

1. [Ed.] See note 1 appended to the Bentley excerpt in Part One, Section 3, above.

Michael Manheim   'Illusion and Kinship'
(1982)

. . . the hostility and the good will [among the play's characters] . . . grows out of the illusions [they] are striving to preserve, but that is not the main point. The main point is that the emotions themselves are authentic and the continuing rhythm of their oscillation, albeit with variations, is assured. Though these figures live at the bottom of civilised human existence, as Larry tells us, they freely feel all the emotions that cluster around hurt and resentment countered by all the emotions that cluster around forgiveness and reconciliation. In short, they feel what everyone feels, their drink serving only to intensify both sets of feelings. This is the point that Hickey misses in his reforming zeal. He fails to see that from the start the illusions these people protect are their means of communication, and that throwing off their illusions will result in nothing more than the perpetual hell of isolation. He also fails to recognise, both in the other characters and in himself, the necessary alternation of hostility and affection. Like most reformers, he wants to cast all hostile reactions out of them, as he supposes he has cast all hostile reactions and all guilt out of himself. Hickey is seeking a utopian existence, and O'Neill now opposes utopias of any sort.

Hickey has in the past served an important purpose in Harry Hope's world. In the past, he has represented a break from the ordinary. But the break has not been a change, really. Hickey has been an extension of the nickel rotgut, more highly charging the pipe dreams and delaying longer the inevitable morning afters. He has allayed the tedium of the old ebbs and flows for a while, and thus has genuinely served to make the saloon-dwellers happier. This time Hickey arrives 'saved', he believes, and determined to 'free' others from their destructive pipe dreams as he feels he has been freed. But in his efforts to get the others to face themselves, he only does more penetratingly what they have been doing all along in their bar-room aggressiveness. He attacks their pipe dreams, and the effect is to make what had usually been said under the protective canopy of raillery become serious. As this happens, real portents of violence begin to be heard. The central pairs begin to disintegrate. There cease to be the regular returns to the reciprocal acceptance that binds them. Moreover, the characters begin to gang up on one another, which we have not seen them do before. The idea of a scapegoat comes into being. We see groups, under pressure to 'face' their illusions, attacking their weaker members as a means of reassuring themselves.

The sickness Hickey comes to cure is for most simply the fear of disappointment and failure all flesh is heir to. To admit one's pipe dreams and to confront one's fears is for Harry Hope and company, as for Relling's 'average man',[1] only to be made miserable, hopeless and alone. The rehabilitation Hickey seeks is not possible. Illusion and kinship for most people go hand in hand – which is not to call kinship an illusion. Kinship is authentic. Most people simply need illusion as a catalyst in achieving it. But there are heroes in the fold, and a hero in O'Neill's later plays is one who can in fact 'face his ghosts', who can live without illusion and in kinship with others. O'Neill is explicit about this in every play onward from *A Touch of the Poet* [written 1939–42; first performed 1957] . . . Larry's stature is larger than the others because he does cast out his fears and his armor of protective illusion, and he has the strength not only to survive but to continue helping others to survive. Hickey is larger yet, in ways we must now examine. Like Larry he lives out a terrible ceremony of emotional exorcism, but Hickey does so aloud, in public, for others to see and learn from. Larry's agony in the Parritt affair is treated throughout as a personal matter, as are his reactions to Parritt's suicide. No one knows, or will ever know, the significance of that falling body but Larry – not even an audience familiar with O'Neill's life and earlier works. But everyone can know and understand what happens to Hickey. Hickey is wrong in what he tries to do for the others, but he is not wrong finally in what he does for himself.

Hickey, misled and misleading, nevertheless finally transcends all others in this play because he most openly and clearly brings together its two affirming energies: the energies of confession and kinship. Confession we have encountered in the many personal confessions throughout O'Neill's works, and kinship we have encountered in the dialogue of genuinely communicating people ever since the 'S. S. Glencairn' series.[1] But we have rarely encountered them together as we do in the character of Hickey, and we have encountered no embodiment of the spirit of human kinship, with all its ebbs and flows starkly in evidence, to rival his. O'Neill through Hickey goes beyond the nihilism of Larry Slade.

Hickey's great confession anticipates Jamie's in *Long Day's Journey* and *A Moon for the Misbegotten* in that he lives out what he is confessing as he confesses it. Hickey starts intending to confess 'everything', and ends up confessing more than he thought was there to confess. In the practised manner of the brilliant raconteur that he is, he builds up slowly to the story of how he came to kill his wife out of love. He thinks he is admitting all the foulness that is in him by recounting the many times and ways he betrayed his wife, always to return and be forgiven. He confirms what he believes to be the totality of his confession by asserting that he came finally to hate her forgivings and her belief in him. But these are all realisations bred by Hickey's not very strong reason, and the 'freedom' he thinks he has achieved by murdering his wife is the muddled pseudo-freedom rationalised confessions lead to. Hickey is not free until the last phrase of his long confession because, though he states that he hated his wife, he has never really come to grips with the reality of that hatred. Even his admission that he killed her to spare her his betrayals is a rationalisation. He killed her because he hated her, pure and simple – and only in reliving this hatred does he understand it for what it is: 'Well, you know what you can do with your pipe dream now, you damned bitch!' He actually has these hateful feelings as he expresses them. But even in expressing them, the realisation is not complete. He must also relive the equally potent feelings of the love which completes his kinship, and this takes place immediately following his famous explosion. As his hatred was great enough to result in his act of ultimate violence, so is his love for her large-scale and authentic:

No! That's a lie! I never said – ! Good god, I couldn't have said that! If I did, I'd gone insane! Why, I loved Evelyn better than anything in life.

And he means it.

Throughout his adult life, Hickey's love and hate had lived inside him – twin feelings, neither of which could ever affect the other. This twinning of opposite, mutually exclusive, feelings is what O'Neill's dialogue of kinship has been revealing and will reveal further about all close human relationships. Who really cares about the cause of Hickey's hatred – the guilt, the envy – or of his love either, for that matter? The facts are simple, that the hate was terribly real, and the love equally so. Only the failure to *recognise* these twin truths breeds the violence: to recognise that authentic love cannot in fact even exist without an accompanying hate. Hickey's tale is an extreme one, but it is through extremes that tragedy has always communicated.

Hickey's doom is the sole tragic irony in this play – because for all the joyous, mock-hypocritical exploitation of his false 'insanity' by the pipe dreamers, Hickey has in fact been insane, as many are insane. He has at a crucial moment lost touch with reality, not because he hated his wife, but because he never acknowledged the inevitability of that hatred. He did not perceive reality because he could not perceive the irreconcilable extremes which govern man's inescapably contradictory nature. The result was the burst of violence by which true tragedy brings things home to us. Hickey is himself ready to die for his crime, not out of guilt so much as for his failure in perception. Like Shakespeare's Gloucester in *King Lear*, he really was blind when he thought he could see. The ever-cerebral Larry – thinking as much of the still-living symbol of his own agony, Parritt, as of Hickey – hopes that 'the Chair' may 'bring him peace at last', but the Hickey led out by the police is already and for the first time actually at peace with himself. He has grown in a moment of deep, sudden recognition, and his growth adds to his already mythic stature. The 'lord of misrule' has become tragic hero. No longer the 'average man', he must *see* where others cannot.

Though Larry Slade is stage-centre at the end of the play, it is the departed Hickey the end of the play celebrates. Hickey's spirit of old – Hickey the bringer of fellowship and good will – governs the saturnalia in which all take part but the benumbed Larry. Hickey has failed in his misguided mission, but he has succeeded in bringing about that kind of release he has always inspired. The celebration we witness at the close of the play is a celebration of the essential Hickey, the Hickey of his previous visits. It is a full, vital expression of the joyful pole of kinship, as the morning after will be the most abysmal expression of its inevitable opposite. The flow of feeling from individual to individual is true, even if it *is* a flow three parts whiskey to one part fellowship. The cacophony which dominates these final festivities, resulting from each person literally 'singing his own song', is an altogether welcome dissonance which tells us that the kinship we have encountered here is real. This clash of songs is one of the few musical images we ever get from O'Neill, but it is a fitting one. The sound is not pleasant, but it is the sound of release – and that is the most satisfying sound of all in the plays of Eugene O'Neill.

In the midst of the festivities Larry sits alone and 'stares oblivious to their racket' – a counter-image, but no more than that. Larry's responses at the end of the play are, as they have always been, cerebral – and cerebral response can lead only to despair in *The Iceman Cometh*. But the party which goes on around him is as much a part of this scene as Larry's ashen detachment. Larry's nihilism cannot be denied; but even Larry acknowledges, by his continuing existence and his abiding loyalty to his 'misbegotten' retinue, that there will be a morning after and that he will have duties to perform. Unlike Parritt, Larry does not *go*.

SOURCE: extract from chapter on the play, in *Eugene O'Neill's New Language of Kinship* (Syracuse, N.Y., 1982), pp. 152–6.

NOTES

1. [Ed.] Dr Relling, in Ibsen's *The Wild Duck*, says that to 'rob the average man of his life-lie' is to rob him of his happiness.

2. [Ed.] See footnote on the 'S. S. Glencairn' plays in the Brooks Atkinson article in this section 3 of Part Two, above.

John H. Raleigh   Mankind   (1965)

[Raleigh has been discussing the issues of freedom and fate, truth and illusion, reality and appearance, in all of O'Neill's plays – Ed.]. . . The great, and most complex, O'Neill play on all these final issues is *The Iceman Cometh* – in many ways his grimmest play of all, concerned as it is with murder, suicide, loneliness, guilt, fear of death, the problems of identity, the necessity for illusions, the ambiguities of pity, the nature of 'truth', and the paradox of commitment.

Like the other late plays it seems to take place on the bottom of the sea. When Wetjoen is described in the opening stage directions, he is said to have '*a suggestion of old authority lurking in him like a memory of the drowned*'. The ships of all the denizens of the saloon, says Larry, 'are long since looted and scuttled and sunk on the bottom' [Act

One]. As in the other late plays, ghosts edge, crab-wise, along the bottom of this sea. Jimmy Tomorrow's speech, for example, has only *'the ghost of a Scotch rhythm in it'*. The over-all dialectic of the play is concerned with the separate but allied problems of reality v. illusion, and commitment v. noncommitment, with reality-commit-ment set off against illusion-noncommitment. The play provides no answers to anything, but states insoluble problems. It says, through most of the characters, that man cannot face reality or commitment, but, through Larry, that he cannot escape from them either; finally however, through Hickey, it says that man probably cannot tell what reality is; he therefore cannot tell either what he should be – or thought he was – committed to. Thus the classic adage to 'Know Thyself' is clearly impossible in this world, although there are several different ways of realising its impossibilities. The only moment of complete self-realisation belongs to Larry at the end of the play, but his is the brute realisation that he is, in truth, only going to die. When the well-intentioned but merciless Hickey tells him in Act Two, 'You'll say to yourself, I'm just an old man who is scared of life, but even more scared of dying. So I'm keeping drunk and hanging on to life at any price, and what of it?' – he is incensed and frightened. At the end of Act Three he says to Hickey, in an ironical and rhetorically defensive manner: 'I'm afraid to live, am I? – and even more afraid to die!' But by the end of the end of the play, having given permission to Parritt to commit suicide, he has finally and completely faced the central fact of life: death. 'Be God, I'm the only real convert to death Hickey has made here. From the bottom of my coward's heart I mean that now!'

If the characters in *The Iceman Cometh* are all faced with the same problems, they do not collectively constitute a democracy with all men equal and of equal value. Rather, like human society itself, they constitute a hierarchy, both as to their worth and as to their function. There is first, and representing mankind in the mass, the majority of the roomers of Harry Hope, the derelict alcoholics; second, there is the outsider and moral leper, Parritt; third, there are the two observers or commentators, Rocky and Larry, who split the world between them in Cervantine fashion, with Rocky playing Sancho Panza and Larry a disillusioned Don Quixote – for, while they are members of the cave-world, they yet can view it with some objectivity. Fourth and finally, there is the reformer and manipulator, Hickey.

To begin with the lowest figure on the moral scale, Parritt, who, of all the haunted, haunting ghosts that people O'Neill's late plays, can never be forgiven and pardoned, even temporarily (as is Jamie

Tyrone in *A Moon for the Misbegotten*). In O'Neill's plays as a whole contemptible people are rare; even murderers – like Christine Mannon in *Mourning Becomes Electra* – are sympathetic and at the end of their lives genuinely pitiable. But there are in the O'Neill world some Smerdyakovs,[1] of which genus Parritt is the most fully drawn. He does, however, have some ancestors: Mrs Rowland in *Before Breakfast* (1916); the shanghaiers in *The Long Voyage Home* (1917); Sweeney and Luke Bentley in *The Rope* (1918); Benny in *Diff'rent* (1920); Hutchins Light in *Dynamo* (1929); and others.

In *The Iceman Cometh* Parritt is unlike anyone else in the play: he is '*unpleasant*', with '*a shifting defiance and ingratiation in his light-blue eyes and an irritating aggressiveness in his manner*'. In the play as a whole O'Neill's stage directions for Parritt have a note of absolute condemnation and moral repulsion that seldom appears elsewhere in his plays. Thus when he confesses to Larry that he betrayed his mother for money to spend on a whore (which is a lie), he is described as having '*the terrible grotesque air, in confessing his sordid baseness, of one who gives an excuse which exonerates him from any real guilt*'. A penny-pincher (perhaps *the* sin against the Holy Ghost in a roomful of thirsty alcoholics), a coward, and a betrayer, out of hatred, of his mother, Parritt has only one mission in life: to get out of it. He is such a moral leper that even that great sinner, Hickey, who can forgive everybody – except himself – cannot even consider absolving Parritt. One of the few times in the play that Hickey becomes genuinely irritated is when Parritt, in Act Four, attempts to identify himself with Hickey, who tells Larry to get rid of him. What Parritt then represents is the unforgivable sin and the complete failure of nerve, with consequent total disintegration of personality. As for his act of betrayal he finally passes judgement on himself when at the end of the play he says to Larry: 'You know I'm really much guiltier than he [Hickey] is. You know what I did is a much worse murder. Because she [Hickey's wife] is dead and yet she [Parritt's mother] has to live.' And, unlike the unsure Hickey, Parritt is certain that he committed his act out of unalloyed hatred. He is thus beyond the pale: 'He's licked, Larry'; 'He's lost all his guts' (Hickey). 'Yuh're a soft old sap, Larry. He's a no-good louse like Hickey. He don't belong' (Rocky). If Larry's realisation is that all men must die, Parritt's is that he, alone, can expiate his crime only by his own immolation. For, morally, O'Neill is an intentionalist, and anything is forgivable except an evil motivation.

The bulk of the characters, however, are not moral lepers, no matter what their past transgressions. But within this group there is a hierarchy as well. The three people whom Hickey wants most to 'save' are Harry, Jimmy Tomorrow and Larry, who are, respectively, the most generous, the most sensitive and the most intelligent of the inhabitants of the cave. The rest constitute a kind of middle class, not too good, not too bad, not too intelligent, not too obtuse. Two of them, Larry and Rocky, are set apart in that, while each has an illusion – Rocky, that he is not a pimp, Larry that he is uncommitted to man and unafraid of death – they are more attached to reality than the rest and they have no illusions about their fellow-inhabitants. They are the 'spokesmen' in the play as a whole, summing up characters and puncturing balloons of fancy, Rocky from his worldly-wise point of view, Larry from his philosophical, or 'foolosophical', one.

Standing outside this world and trying to manipulate it is Hickey who – like so many of O'Neill's characters at the climacteric and at the end of their lives – has become his own father, the preacher, who shows the way, or purports to show the way, to salvation. Besides being the most ambiguous character in the play, in his dual role as murderer-reformer, Hickey stands in a completely different sphere from the other characters (although, in a much less clear-cut way Parritt is in this same sphere). First, Hickey has just murdered someone and is accordingly himself facing death. Thus, while most of the others live on illusions, he is living on the most powerful, elemental and terrifying of realities: the memory of a murder and the expectation of extinction (Parritt has not committed an actual murder and does not know he is going to die until the end of the play). Thus Hickey is in possession of certain certainties although, characteristically, O'Neill takes these certain certainties away from him by the end of the play, leaving the meaning of the play, in Larry's phrase, 'all question and no answer'.

The two things that the inhabitants of Harry Hope's fear the most are two realities: a time-sequence and the light of day. Hickey is the bringer of both. Most of the characters in the play have no sense of temporality, immersed as they are in a glorified past: 'Isn't a pipe dream of yesterday a touching thing?' And vaguely ruminating about an impossible future, 'The tomorrow movement is a sad and beautiful thing, too'. The present, then, is an endless repetition, every day precisely like the day before and the day to come: drink, talk, memories, dreams, and the final annihilation of drunken sleep. Only death, which is unthinkable (except for Larry at the end), could alter the sequence and reintroduce a real past and a real future. But such is not the case with Hickey who is facing not only reality, but a real past and a real future. He thus can think in terms of change. He seems in fact to some of the others to exist in another world from theirs, a world not only real but inhumanly so. As Parritt says, 'There's something not human behind his damned grinning and kidding'.

Moreover, Hickey's sense of time is extraordinarily heightened by his own situation. For while he is facing extinction and thinks he has not much time at his disposal, actually his moment-by-moment sense of time has been enormously expanded, so much so that only a few hours, he thinks, will suffice to 'reform' the barnacle-encrusted inhabitants of Harry Hope's. According to Dostoevsky, who knew what he was talking about in these matters, the imminence of death has the effect of greatly enlarging the content of time. At the beginning of *The Idiot* Prince Myshkin tells what must have been Dostoevsky's own psychological experience when he faced a firing squad in 1849. Myshkin tells of a man, under sentence of death for a political offence, who is led out to the scaffold. Twenty minutes later a reprieve was read and another punishment was passed on the prisoners. The man later said he would never forget those twenty minutes because they were so full. When the time was down to five minutes, the same feeling persisted: 'He told me that those five minutes seemed to him an infinite time, a vast wealth; he felt that he has so many lives left in those five minutes that there was no need yet to think of the last moment' [ch. 5, Garnett translation]. Down to two minutes he still felt mentally omnipotent: he thought of existence and non-existence and the relationship between the two: 'He meant to decide all that in those two minutes!' It is this apocalyptical sense that sustains Hickey in the face of all his lack of success and the churlishness of his reformees, and makes him feel God-like in his omniscience and omnipotence as he bustles around in his role as Saviour: 'He's been hoppin' from room to room all night. Yuh can't stop him. He's got his Reform Wave goin' strong this mornin'!' says Rocky in Act Three.

If Hickey would push them back into a genuine time sequence, he would also thrust them into the light of the sun, for the morning of 'reform' day is hot and sunny although the sunlight itself barely penetrates the recesses of The Last Chance Saloon. Here then, at the heart of the play, is O'Neill's own ironical dramatisation of Plato's parable of the cave, in which the philosopher drags protesting mankind – content to live in semi-darkness, satisfied with his own ignorance, never knowing the real nature of anything – out into the bright and merciless light of the sun. Only, in O'Neill's play, the philosopher is a salesman who has just committed a murder and 'mankind' is a motley collection of alcoholic derelicts. The point, however, of both Plato and O'Neill is identical: eyes accustomed to darkness do not want to see the light: 'And suppose', says Plato, 'once more that he [man] is reluctantly dragged up a steep and rugged ascent, and held fast until he is forced into the presence of the sun himself, is he not likely to be pained and irritated? When he approaches the light his eyes will be dazzled, and he will not be able to see anything at all of what are now called realities' [*The Republic* Bk VII, Jowett translation]. Thus the '*blind*' Harry Hope forces himself out into the sunlight but scurries right back, as do the others at greater leisure.

One of the pleasures of the darkened cave is that in it nothing is quite certain or clear-cut, even the names of objects. As Plato says of the inhabitants of the cave, '. . . if they were able to converse with one another, would they not suppose that they were naming what was actually before them?' And they would, of course, be misnaming everything.

So in *The Iceman Cometh* names are both highly important and highly problematical. Like the blind, or like primitive man, the characters can only perceive something by attaching a name to it; but the name, like its object, is often shifting and ambiguous in meaning. The ambiguous but all-important question of nomenclature is carried throughout the play by two of its sustaining jokes: Larry as the old 'Foolosopher' (fool and/or philosopher); whether Pearl and Margie are 'tarts' or 'whores'. Names take on an almost totemistic power: you are what you are called (although you may not be in truth what you are called). Furthermore, there is a kind of insane 'logic' operating about names. They are like assumptions in a mathematical equation: given one name, other names must follow. Thus Pearl to Rocky: 'Aw right, Rocky. We're whores. You know what dat makes you, don't you?' Margie: 'A lousy little pimp, dat's what.' Pearl: 'A dirty little Ginny pimp, dat's what!' This name-calling orgy of derogation spreads out to include his race as well: 'yuh poor little Ginny', 'yuh little Wop!' But when the reconciliation occurs at the end of the play, after Hickey's departure, Rocky becomes once more, 'Our little bar-tender' and 'a cute little Ginny at dat!'. The ambiguities of the various appelations of Joe Mott, the 'black' man who is morally 'white', likewise run throughout the play. A 'dinge', a 'black bastard', a 'doity nigger' when the others are enraged at him, he is a 'white' man in the stretches of peace.

The point is, of course, that no one is quite sure who or what he or she is, and the single most ironical speech in the play is, appropriately, Joe Mott's: 'Don't you get it in your heads I's pretendin' to be what I ain't, or dat I ain't proud to be what I is, get me?' As in so many major documents by major American writers, some – in this case most – of the characters in the play have deep-set doubts about their own identity.

Moreover, Hickey's panacea for the discovery of the true self and the real identity by destroying both the past and the future is deeply dubious as well: 'You'll be in a today where there is no yesterday or tomorrow to worry you'. 'No', says Larry to Rocky in Act Four, 'it doesn't look good, Rocky. I mean, the peace Hickey's brought you. It isn't contented enough, if you have to make everyone else a pimp, too.' And as they all cry out, after having been jarred back into a time sequence, seen the sun, inspected reality, and destroyed the lies about the past and smashed the daydreams of the future: 'We can't pass out! And you promised us peace!'

For Hickey's 'message' is, as Larry says in Act Two, equivocal: 'Be God, its a second feast of Belshazzar, with Hickey to do the writing on the wall'. But there is no Daniel to interpret the cabalistic hieroglyphics. In so far as Hickey's 'message' is understandable or realisable, it is wholly negative and destructive, despite its admonition to face the 'truth'. Again Larry gives the key: 'Be God, it's not to Bakunin's ghost you ought to pray in your dreams, but to the great Nihilist, Hickey! He's started a movement that'll blow up the world!'. As the historical Nihilists would have destroyed the past of mankind, Hickey would destroy the past of the individuals in the play. By Act Four, he himself is apprehensive of his own 'cure' and is nervously exhorting the depressed patients to be content: 'Can't you see there is no tomorrow now? You're rid of it forever! You've killed it! You don't have to give a damn about anything any more!' But man needs his past and his future, no matter how illusory, for he is incurably lonely. In Lazarus's millennium there will be no more loneliness: 'Lonely no more! Man's loneliness is but his fear of life! Lonely no more! Millions of laughing stars are around me!' [*Lazarus Laughed*, Three, 2]. But the human condition, before this millennium, is inescapably solitary, more so as one gets older. This is why the elderly talk and confide; they can no longer endure being locked up with their own secrets. As Tiberius describes the phenomenon to Lazarus, the old must talk because they cannot bear their own solitude. And the loneliness is always fearful. In *Strange Interlude* when Darrell meets Marsden and speculates why a man of Marsden's intelligence and talent does not go deeper into the problems of human existence in his novels, he concludes that Marsden is afraid to, 'afraid he'll meet himself somewhere'. Very often man's only companions are his own past and his own future, chimerical as they may be. . . .

SOURCE: extract from chapter ('Mankind') in *The Plays of Eugene O'Neill* (Carbondale, Ill., 1965), pp. 161–9.

NOTE

1. [Ed.] Smerdyakov: a repulsive character in Dostoyevsky's *The Brothers Karamazov*.

PART THREE

Long Day's Journey Into Night

1. COMMENT BY CARLOTTA & EUGENE O'NEILL

I   'IT WAS A THING THAT HAUNTED HIM'   (1956)

. . . *Long Day's Journey Into Night* . . . was already taking shape in his mind as he worked on *The Iceman*. Carlotta [his wife] had first learned of the project one night in June 1939. 'Whenever Gene was very upset about something or nervous', she has recalled, 'he would come to my bedroom or call me to his and talk himself out. This night he told me he was going to write a play about his family. It was a thing that haunted him. He was *bedeviled* into writing it. . . . He had to get it out of his system, he had to forgive whatever it was that caused this tragedy between himself and his mother and father.

'He talked all night – it was like talking to himself. I shut up and didn't say a word. He said, "I've *got* to write this. I'm afraid someone might find out about us one day and write something vulgar and melodramatic about it, even make a play out of it. But it was never vulgar! Even if my father was miserly, even if my mother used to take drugs whenever things got too much for her, even if my brother spent so much of his time in whorehouses."

'In the evenings we used to sit before the fireplace, and I remember one night when Gene, staring into the fire, said, "I'm just thinking of the hell every member of the family went through – separately."

'When he started *Long Day's Journey* it was a most strange experience to watch that man being tortured every day by his own writing. He would come out of his study at the end of a day gaunt and sometimes weeping. His eyes would be all red and he looked ten years older than when he went in in the morning.' . . .

SOURCE: extract from Louis Sheaffer, *O'Neill: Son and Artist* (Boston, Mass., 1973); p. 505 – incorporating material from Seymour Peck, 'Talking with Mrs O'Neill', interview–article in the *New York Times* (4 Nov. 1956). For more details of Mrs O'Neill's impressions at this period, see Travis Bogard's contribution in section 3 of this Part Three, below.

II   'A DEEPLY TRAGIC PLAY'   (1940)

. . . From the start of its composition, O'Neill had the general plan for *Long Day's Journey* clear in his mind. Without disclosing that it was autobiographical, he had told Nathan [in 1940], after finishing the first act, that the play would cover one day in a family's life, 'a day in which things occur which evoke the whole past of the family and reveal every aspect of its interrelationships. A deeply tragic play, but without any violent dramatic action. At the final curtain, there they still are, trapped within each other by the past, each guilty and at the same time innocent, scorning, loving, pitying each other, understanding and yet not understanding at all, forgiving but still doomed never to be able to forget.' . . .

SOURCE: extract from letter to G. J. Nathan, in Louis Sheaffer, op. cit., p. 509.

2. COMMENTATORS ON THE 1956 & 1958 PRODUCTIONS

John Chapman (1956)

'O'Neill's Most Beautiful Play'

Let us now forget something that everybody knows by now, that Eugene O'Neill's *Long Day's Journey Into Night* is about himself, his parents and his brother. This is a mere detail, for the drama could have been written and very possibly was written about anybody else. The news this morning is that *Long Day's Journey Into Night* is a magnificent work, and last evening it was given a magnificent performance by Florence Eldridge, Fredric March, Jason Robards and Bradford Dillman. It exploded like a dazzling skyrocket over the humdrum of Broadway theatricals.

This is O'Neill's most beautiful play – perhaps the only beautiful one he ever wrote. And it is one of the great dramas of any time. In one speech, the tubercular young man who is supposed to be O'Neill declines to be cheered when he is told that he has the makings of a poet. He answers that he is like a bum who has asked for a cigarette: he doesn't have the makings but only the habit. In this, his next-to-last play, O'Neill, who so often yearned beyond his reach, became a poet.

It is a long play, running for about three and half hours, and one's attention may wander for a minute here and there. But the attention will not wander for long, because the profound compassion of the writing and the superb rightness of the acting cannot long be ignored.

A summary of the plot seems dismal enough to discourage all but the bravest playgoers from venturing into the Helen Hayes Theatre. There are a father and mother and two sons. The father, a noted actor, is a drunk and a miser. The mother is a sweet dope fiend. The elder brother is a cynical sot and the younger one is a sick and troubled boy.

It is this younger son who says, 'If you don't make allowances in this family you'll go nuts'. And it is these allowances – the allowances O'Neill made out of the great depths of his sympathy – which make *Long Day's Journey Into Night* the great cleansing emotional experience that it is.

One by one, the four people in this family try gropingly to explain how and why they became the way they are. Says one of them: 'The things life has done to us we cannot excuse or explain. The past is the present. It's the future, too'. All have been caught in a destiny they cannot alter.

As they tell of themselves, each in a long monologue, these people become larger than their own small lives; they become humanity, looking for something but not knowing exactly what it is looking for. They are magnificent.

And the performances, under the direction of José Quintero, are magnificent. Miss Eldridge reaches stunning heights in the art of acting, and so do March as her actor-husband, Robards as their hopeless and drunken son, and Dillman, the sick one with the touch of the poet in him – who is, of course, the young O'Neill who had only begun to write.

Last evening at the Helen Hayes was a great evening for the American theatre, and the first-night audience was spellbound and enraptured.

SOURCE: review ('A Drama of Sheer Magnificence') of the opening performance at the Helen Hayes Theatre, 7 November 1956, in the *New York Daily News* (8 Nov. 1956).

Walter Kerr   (1956)

'A Stunning Theatrical Experience'

In *Long Day's Journey Into Night*, Florence Eldridge plays a shattered mother – her white hair drifting about the damaged prettiness of her face – who has convinced herself, with the help of morphine, that her arthritic hands are the true cause of all her pain. She stretches them out before her in the blurred light of a foggy seaside afternoon and exults 'They can't touch me now – I see them, but they're far away! The pain is gone'.

This, I think, is what Eugene was doing when he put to paper the searing and sorry record of the wreck of his family. He has held up his mother, father and his brother at the arm's length of the stage, looking at everything that was ugly and misshapen and destroyed in them, and now the pain is gone.

It is gone, too. Though the four-hour, endlessly savage examination of conscience on the stage of the Helen Hayes is deliberately, masochistically harrowing in the ferocity of its revelation, the agony that O'Neill felt whenever he contemplated his own beginnings is not passed onto his audience. It is in some curious and even exalting manner exorcised, washed away, leaving in its place an undefined dignity, an agreed-upon peace, a powerful sense of exhilarated completion.

Long Day's Journey is not a play. It is a lacerating round-robin of recrimination, self-dramatisation, lies that deceive no one, confessions that never expiate the crime. Around the whiskey bottles and the tattered leather chairs and the dangling light-cords that infest the decaying summer home of the Tyrones (read O'Neills), a family of ghosts sit in a perpetual game of four-handed solitaire, stir to their feet in a danse macabre that outlines the geography of Hell, place themselves finally on an operating table that allows for no anesthetic. When the light falls they are still – but not saved.

How has O'Neill kept self-pity and vulgarity and cheap bravado out of this prolonged, unasked-for, improbable inferno? Partly by the grim determination that made him a major dramatist: the insistence that the roaring fire he could build by grinding his own two hands together was the fire of truth. You can disbelieve, but you cannot deny him his heat, his absolute passion.

And partly by a talent he must have picked up from that greedy and grandiose father of his: a talent that puts words together so that actors can chew them, spit them, tear at one another's skins with them. Director José Quintero has seen to it that everyone of his present players knows how to handle that whip.

Fredric March cracks down on the skinflint monarch that O'Neill remembered as his father with majestic authority from the outset. Laughing a bit too much and a bit too hollowly, working off his nerves with a restless cigar, snapping every insult like a guilty bulldog, he foreshadows the whole sodden fantasia of the midnight to come. When he reaches that last grim débâcle, and is forced to stumble to his feet in a slavering but heart-breaking tribute to his lost glory, he is in every way superb.

Hot on his heels is Jason Robards Jnr as the dissolute elder brother who may have led the consumptive Edmund (read Eugene) into every sort of vice to help square away his own failure. Mr

Robards lurches into the final scene with his hands, his mouth, and his mind wildly out of control, cracks himself in two as he pours out every tasteless truth that is in him, and subsides at last into the boozy sleep of the damned. The passage is magnificent.

Florence Eldridge makes the downward course of an incapable mother utterly intelligible. She does not have the deep, resonant notes that will sustain her woman through the blinding, tragic memories of the center of the play; she cannot quite fight fury with fury. Yet there is a hidden delicacy that is often touching in the shallow gayeties and transparent pretences of a convent girl who could not survive the world.

Bradford Dillman handles the exceedingly difficult and soul-searching soliloquies of his poet who 'didn't have the makings, just the habit' with swift, sensitive skill, and Katherine Ross is excellent in the brief role of 'second girl' who is permitted to tipple while her mistress mourns. The David Hays setting is a perfect echo – curving and empty – of the universe these characters wander.

For any one who cares about the American theater, *Long Day's Journey* is, of course, an obligation. But it is more than that. It is a stunning theatrical experience.

SOURCE: review of the opening performance, 7 November 1956, in the *New York Herald Tribune* (8 Nov. 1956).

Kenneth Tynan   (1958)

'Expecting to Hear a Playwright, One Meets a Man'

Eugene O'Neill died five years ago. The eclipse of reputation that commonly befalls great men as soon as they die has not yet happened to him; and now that *Long Day's Journey Into Night* has followed *The Iceman Cometh* into London, I doubt if it ever will. O'Neill has conquered. We have the measure of him at last, and it is vast indeed. His work stretches like a mountain range across more than three decades, rising at the end to these two tenebrous peaks, in which the nature of his immense, hard-pressed talent most clearly reveals itself. As Johnson said of Milton, he could not carve heads upon cherry-stones; but he could cut a colossus from a rock. Sometimes the huge groups of his imagination stayed stubbornly buried within the rock; worse, they would sometimes emerge lopsided and unwieldly, so that people smiled at them – not without reason, for it is widely felt that there is nothing funnier than a deformed giant.

Many charges, during his lifetime, were levelled at O'Neill by the cherry-stone connoisseurs of criticism. That he could not think; that he was no poet; that his attempts at comedy were even more pathetic than his aspirations to tragedy. The odd thing is that all of these charges are entirely true. The defence admits them: it does not wish even to cross-examine the witnesses. Their testimony, which would be enough to annihilate most other playwrights, is in O'Neill's case irrelevant. His strength lies elsewhere. It has nothing to do with intellect, verbal beauty, or the accepted definitions of tragedy and comedy. It exists independently of them: indeed, they might even have cramped and depleted it.

What is this strength, this durable virtue? I got the clue to it from the American critic Stark Young, into whose reviews I have lately been dipping [*Immortal Shadows* (1948); see the excerpt in Part One, section 2, above – Ed.]. Mr Young is sometimes a windy writer, but the wind is usually blowing in the right direction. As early as 1926 he saw that O'Neill's theatrical power did not arise from any 'strong dramatic expertness', but that 'what moved us was the *cost to the dramatist of what he handled'*. (My italics.) Two years later, reviewing *Dynamo*, he developed this idea. He found in the play an 'individual poignancy' to which he responded no matter how tritely or unevenly it was expressed. From this it was a short step to the truth. 'Even when we are not at all touched by the feeling itself or the idea presented', he wrote, 'we are stabbed to our depths by the importance of this feeling to him, and we are all his, not because of what he says but because saying it meant so much to him'.

Thirty years later we are stabbed in the same way, and for the same reason. The writing of *Long Day's Journey* must have cost O'Neill more than Mr Young could ever have conceived, for its subject is that rarest and most painful of all *dramatis personae*, the dramatist himself. No more honest or unsparing autobiographical play exists in dramatic literature. Yet what grips us about it is not the craft of a playwright. It is the need, the vital, driving plaint, of a human being.

We are watching a crucial day in O'Neill's late youth, covered with a thin gauze of fiction; events are telescoped, and the family's name is Tyrone. They live in a gaunt, loveless New England house. Father is a rich retired actor, now beetle-browed with drink, whose upbringing as an immigrant Irish pauper has made him a miser: he recognises the fault, but cannot cure it. His wife suffered badly at the birth of their second son (Edmund, otherwise Eugene), and he hired a cheap quack to ease her pain, with the result that she has become a morphine addict. The elder boy is a failed actor, something of a whoremaster, and a great deal of a drunk. His brother, Edmund, who has been to sea and is ambitious to be a poet, also drinks and detests more than he wholesomely should.

We catch the quartet on the desperate day when mother, after a long abstinence, returns to drugs, and Edmund learns that he has TB. With these urgent, terrible realities the family cannot cope. Old rows, old resentments keep boiling up; the pressures and recriminations of the past will not let the present live. Every conversation leads inexorably to the utterance of some sudden, unforgivable, scab-tearing cruelty. At every turn O'Neill points the contrast between official Irish-Catholic morality and the sordid facts of drink and dope. The family goes round and round in that worst of domestic rituals, the Blame Game. I blame my agony on you; you blame yours on her; she blames hers on me. Father blames his past; mother blames father; elder son blames both, and younger son blames all of them. If the play has a flaw, it is that O'Neill, the younger son, lets nobody blame him – though I recall, as I write this, the moment when his mother cries out that she would not be what she is had he never been born. The wheel, coming full circle, runs over all of them. Shortly after the events covered in the play, O'Neill entered a sanatorium, where, he wrote later, 'the urge to write first came to me'. It was more than an urge, it was a compulsion.

The London production is much shorter than those I saw in Berlin and New York; about a quarter of the text has been cut away. This is shrewd pruning, since a non-American English-speaking cast might not have been able to carry the full four-hour burden. Alan Bates, shock-haired and forlorn, approaches Edmund with just the right abandon. Once inside the part, however, he stumbles over a distracting North Country accent. Ian Bannen, on the other hand, gets easily to the heart of the elder brother, especially in the last-act debauch when he confesses to Edmund how much he hates and envies him: what he lacks is the exterior of the seedy Broadway masher. He falls short of his New York counterpart, Jason Robards Jnr, just as far as Anthony Quayle falls short of Fredric March. Mr March, with his corrugated face and burning eyes, looked as weighty as if he were made of iron. Mr Quayle, though he conveys every syllable of the part's meaning, never seems to be heavier than tin.

By West End standards, let me add, all these performances are exceptionally good. That of Gwen Ffrangçon-Davies is by any standards magnificent. In this production mother is the central figure: a guileful, silver-topped doll, her hands clenched by rheumatism into claws, her voice drooping except when drugs tighten it into a tingling, bird-like, tight-rope brightness. Her sons stare at her, and she knows why they are staring, but: 'Is my hair coming down?' she pipes, warding off the truth with a defensive flirtatiousness. At the end, when the men are slumped in a stupor, she tells us in a delicate quaver how the whole mess began. 'Then I married James Tyrone, and I was happy for a time. . . .' The curtain falls on a stupendous evening. One goes expecting to hear a playwright, and one meets a man.

SOURCE: review of the first London production, at the Globe Theatre, in the *Observer* (28 Sept. 1958); reproduced in Tynan's *A View of the English Stage* (London, 1975), pp. 229–32.

152

3. CRITICAL STUDIES

Frederic I. Carpenter 'The Climax of O'Neill's Development' (1979)

... *Long Day's Journey* marks the climax of O'Neill's development, both psychological and artistic. From the beginning of his career he had attempted to transmute his autobiographical experiences into art: *Exorcism* (1920), *The Straw* (1921) and *Welded* (1924) had all described the artist as hero; but all had failed, either because of sentimentality or because of idealisation. In 1928 he had consciously projected an autobiographical work as his 'grand opus'. And now, twelve years later, he realised this lifelong ambition with the writing of *Long Day's Journey*. During these years he had effectively purged himself of his former pride and self-pity. And on completing the play, he recognised it, objectively, as his masterpiece.

After writing *Long Day's Journey*, O'Neill stipulated that it should not be produced until twenty-five years after his death. But in 1950, after the death of Eugene Jnr, he relented somewhat, and in 1956 his widow approved its publication and production. The Royal Dramatic Theatre of Stockholm was awarded first rights because O'Neill had been impressed by earlier Swedish productions of his plays and had been disappointed by the American reception of *The Iceman* and *A Moon*. But *Long Day's Journey* achieved immediate critical praise and popular success with both the Swedish and American productions. Although some critics complained of its length and its unrelieved pessimism, the majority was enthusiastic. And many, who had formerly disliked O'Neill, admired this play. Stephen Whicher witnessed its Swedish première, and, although 'starting with a prejudice against O'Neill',[1] was impressed both by the play and by the fascinated attention of the audience throughout its four and a half hours on the stage. In America most serious critics were enthusiastic. And T. S. Eliot gave testimony to an enthusiasm which he had not felt for the earlier dramas of the author. Since then the play's reputation has steadily increased. And the moving picture version, which follows the text closely, achieved further success.

The reasons for the excellence of *Long Day's Journey* are not immediately apparent. Its style approximates Edmund Tyrone's description: 'It will be faithful realism, at least'. But the realism achieves a transcendence unequalled in the earlier dramas, and it is 'faithful' not to the letter but to the spirit of its autobiographical materials. The story of Edmund Tyrone and his family is essentially the story of the young O'Neill. But the illumination which flashes through it, like the beams from the lighthouse through the fog, is that achieved only by the mature playwright.

Perhaps *Long Day's Journey* is most remarkable for what it is not. It is not a drama of action: 'It austerely ignores almost every means, including action, by which the usual play interests an audience'.[2] And it is not a drama of violence: although the emotions involved find violent expression in words, they remain within the bounds of 'normal' family life. It is not, therefore, a drama of extremes: the 'Lower Depths' of *The Iceman* and the domestic depravity of *Mourning Becomes Electra* have been left behind; and the mystical ecstasy of *Lazarus Laughed* appears only as a remembrance of things past. *Long Day's Journey* describes the mid-world of middle-class family life, and its greatness lies in its simple domestication both of tragic emotion and of human insight. The impact of the mother's dope addiction is intensified by the very fact that there is no 'abnormal' reason for it. And, when in the last act, the father thoughtlessly denounces Dante Gabriel Rossetti as a 'dope-fiend', the irony becomes obvious.

The positive excellence of the play consists not in the plot but in the characterisation. The four chief characters are probably the four most memorable in all O'Neill's works – with the addition of Ephraim Cabot in *Desire Under the Elms*. The father embodies the qualities of petty dictator characteristic of all O'Neill's fathers, but he remains more human and more understandable. Mary Tyrone embodies the qualities of unworldly innocence typical both of American womanhood of the nineteenth century and of all Christian mariolatry as well – as her name suggests. Jamie Tyrone reincarnates the Mephistopheles of Dion Anthony, but without the artificiality of a mask. And Edmund Tyrone, seemingly passive, develops steadily, although unobtrusively, during the play until at the end he achieves what O'Neill had prophesied for his autobiographical hero: 'the birth of a soul'.

Although *Long Day's Journey* abjures physical action, it dramatises psychological action to a superlative degree. Mary Tyrone gradually regresses from the sunlight world of reality to the fog-bound world of dope and dreams. As the play begins, she *'smiles affectionately'*; but, as it ends *'she stares before her in a sad dream'*. But her son Edmund, in almost perfect counterpoint, begins as 'mama's baby, papa's pet', and ends as the only member of the family wholly clear headed and emotionally unwarped. For him – as for the author and the audience – the play has been 'a play of discovery, like Oedipus'. And for Edmund Tyrone the commitment to the sanatorium will provide a release from the family furies and ultimately a 'journey into light'.

Meanwhile Edmund Tyrone's psychological journey into light is motivated by his conflicts with – and his final understanding of – both his father and his brother. At first he and Jamie make common cause against the tyranny of the father, and the first part of the play dramatises their guerrilla warfare against his miserliness and his pompous self-importance. 'Old Gaspard, the miser' and 'the Beautiful Voice' stand between them and (as they believe) happiness and self-fulfilment. But in the final act James Tyrone explains to Edmund the ancestral causes of his miserliness and his theatrical manner, and Edmund *'Moved, stares at his father with understanding – slowly.* "I'm glad you've told me this, Papa. I know you a lot better now".' The sources of his conflict with his father have been clarified, and Edmund begins to see the light.

But the conflict of father and son – which seems to be the source of Edmund's confusion and which the father's confession illuminates so clearly – is not the true source of the tragedy, nor does it make the climax of the play. The conflict of Edmund with his brother Jamie is much more fundamental, more subtle, and more significant. And the discovery of the sources of this conflict – indeed, the very discovery that this conflict exists at all – marks the true climax of the play. It provides the final moment of illumination, and of tragic catharsis. In the last act, after the confessions of the father and of Edmund, Jamie comes home drunk. And after a comic account of his maudlin evening with 'Fat Violet', he suddenly tells Edmund what 'I don't want to hear –'. In a burst of drunken self-revelation he explains to his brother the subconscious cause of Edmund's 'consumption'. Jamie – the jealous older brother, the cynical tempter of innocent youth, Pan, Mephistopheles, Cain – explains why, subconsciously, he has sought to kill the life-giving illusions of his younger brother.

This conflict of older brother with younger – of Cain with Abel, of cynical materialist with aspiring artist – goes far beyond any simple conflict of character. It illuminates the conflict of two philosophies of life – two philosophies which *seem* the same; which James Tyrone, Snr, believes to be the same; and which many critics of O'Neill have believed to be identical. The conflict between the cynical negations preached by Jamie and the tragic transcendence of these negations, which lies at the heart of all Edmund Tyrone's

(Eugene O'Neill's) dramas, is, indeed, the subject finally illuminated by *Long Day's Journey*.

Sophus Winther has pointed out that the poetic philosophy of the autobiographical Edmund Tyrone constitutes one of the main themes of the drama.[3] By far the most 'literary' of O'Neill's plays, it contains many passages of quotation from O'Neill's favorite authors and it even includes several lists of these authors, both in its stage directions and in the dialogue itself. And the greatest – indeed, the only – criticism of Edmund voiced by his father, concerns the 'rotten' books which he reads: 'That damned library of yours: Voltaire, Rousseau, Schopenhauer, Nietzsche, Ibsen! Atheists, fools, and madmen! And your poets! This Dowson, and this Baudelaire, and Swinburne, and Oscar Wilde, and Whitman and Poe! Whoremongers and degenerates! Pah!' The father emphasises that he considers Edmund's philosophy to be as 'degenerate' as Jamie's: 'There's little choice between the philosophy you learned from Broadway loafers, and the one Edmund got from his books'.

But just before this wholesale condemnation, by the father, of the evil 'philosophy' of both sons, Edmund had attacked Jamie. '*Parodying his brother's cynicism*', he had exclaimed: 'Christ, if I felt the way you do – !' And Jamie had replied: 'I thought you did. Your poetry isn't very cheery.' Thus Edmund had emphasised his rejection of his brother's cynicism as early as the second act, and his brother had pretended surprise. But in the last act, Jamie, drunk, explains the subconscious causes of his difference from Edmund, and he confesses that he had led Edmund into temptation on purpose, to make him fall: 'Made getting drunk romantic. Made whores fascinating vampires instead of poor, stupid, diseased slobs they really are.' By emphasising the radical difference between his own mephistophelian cynicism and Edmund's genuine tragic idealism, Jamie clarifies the values and the meaning of the play.

This emphatic statement of the difference between the evil of Jamie and the good of Edmund is doubly important because it clarifies the apparent confusion between good and evil suggested by Larry Slade's rejection of 'truth' in *The Iceman*. There is as radical a difference between the 'drunkenness' of Jamie and that of Edmund as there is between the romantic philosophies of despair and of transcendence. And, when Edmund recounts to his father 'some high spots' of his memories, he emphasises his own mystical experiences: 'I became drunk with the beauty and singing rhythm of it, and for a moment I lost myself – actually lost my life. I was set free!' In this moment of transcendence he experienced 'the birth of a soul', which would result in his ultimate triumph. And he then felt closer to his father – who had experienced similar moments of triumph but had forgotten them – than he did to his brother, who had always remained lost in the night.

The psychological 'long day's journey into night', which gives title and direction to the play, is a different journey for each of its characters. For the mother, it is a sad journey into the fog of dope and dream. For Jamie, it is a hopeless journey into the night of cynicism and despair. For the father, it is a tragic journey down the wrong road, away from an earlier triumph. But for Edmund, it is, prophetically, a journey beyond night. And dramatically, the story of these conflicting characters and of their contrasting journeys is the essence of the play.

But, philosophically, the play focuses on the Transcendental idealism of Edmund Tyrone. And his tragedy is not that of defeat, but of a suffering which leads to illumination. Like the others, he also journeys through the fog and the night. But, unlike them, he has seen – and will again see – beyond the illusions which surround him. And ideally the play reaches its climax in his eloquent account of his own experiences of transcendence, ending with a metaphor of illumination not unlike that of Emerson's famous essay on 'Illusions': '. . . Then the moment of ecstatic freedom came. The peace, the end of the quest, the last harbor, the joy of belonging. . . . Like a saint's vision of beatitude. Like the veil of things as they seem drawn back by an unseen hand. For a second you see – and seeing the secret, are the secret. For a second there is meaning! Then the hand lets the veil fall and you are alone, lost in the fog again. . . .' Even if only 'for a second', there has been the experience of meaning. . . .

Source: extract from chapter ('The Final Plays') in *Eugene O'Neill*, 'Twayne American Authors' series (Boston, Mass., 1979), pp. 154–9.

NOTES

[Reorganised and renumbered from the original – Ed.]

1. Stephen Whicher, 'O'Neill's Long Journey', *Commonweal*, LXIII (16 March 1956), pp. 614–15.
2. Ibid.
3. Sophus Winther, 'O'Neill's Tragic Themes', *Arizona Quarterly*, XIII (Winter 1957), pp. 295–307.

Travis Bogard   The Door and the Mirror
(1972)

. . . Mrs O'Neill's diary for 21 June 1939 contains what is possibly
the first recorded mention of another play he planned whose subject
was his family and whose title was *Long Day's Journey Into Night*. The
play was begun shortly after the completion of *The Iceman Cometh*
and, together with *Hughie*, was O'Neill's major creative effort of
1940. It was completed in September. Then, after a period of illness,
he turned to its sequel, *A Moon for the Misbegotten*. He had written
half of the first draft of that play when the Japanese bombed Pearl
Harbor. O'Neill wrote to Dudley Nichols on 16 December 1941 that
he had managed to finish the draft, but that the heart had gone out
of its writing. Although he worked on it sporadically through 1943
and during the same period made revisions of *A Touch of the Poet*
and developed the scenario of *The Last Conquest*, O'Neill's career as
a playwright ended as the United States entered the war. By 1943,
the tremor in his hand made sustained work impossible.

His illness and the war were real reasons for silence, but equally
important was an underlying cause: having written the two plays
about his family, O'Neill had no further place to go. *Long Day's
Journey Into Night* was the play he had been trying to write from the
outset of his career; its achievement was his raison d'être as an
artist. *A Moon for the Misbegotten* was an essential coda, an act of
love, of charity and of contrition. . . .

. . . Both plays begin in the full light of day to the sound of
laughter. In *Long Day's Journey Into Night*, as the Tyrones enter from
the dining room, laughter sounds gently. Sun pours through the
windows, the fog and the sound of the foghorn that has kept the
family awake through the night have gone. The moment is poised
and normal, but almost at once O'Neill denies its normality and
starts the progression that had been a hallmark of his style from the
first work he did for the theatre. The light dwindles, the fog returns,
the foghorn sounds again. Gradually, the space diminishes to the
area defined by a single light-bulb over the central table in the
room. The Tyrone's world is seen in its barest essentials. The
proposition is clear, both to the actors and their characters: if life is
to be created it must be evolved from the simple elements in this
limited space. There are no extraneous symbols – isolating actors
in follow-spots, diminishing the room by pulling in the walls of the
set. Everything is in the action as the fog becomes the physical
evidence of the isolation of the Tyrones.

The view of human nature set forth in the plays is of divided beings – the conception that earlier occasioned O'Neill's use of masks and other devices to suggest outer and inner lives. The Tyrones, however, need no masks. In their nearly mortal extremity, they have nothing to hide. Their pain fills their being so completely that their essential natures lie close to the surface. Thus Tyrone's charm, his friendliness and grace have worn thin under the erosion of despair. His actor's carriage and voice are ingrained in his demeanor, but as the night wears on and as the whiskey sickens him without making him drunk, the hidden man comes clearly into view. Jamie's cynical mask is dropped as the whiskey begins to talk, permitting the defenceless child in him to be seen. In the same way, as Mary descends further into the doped state, the young girl alive within the pain-wracked woman comes forth to haunt them all. Whiskey and morphine effectively remove all disguise.

The words that come when the masks are off are in the form of soliloquies and monologues such as were from the first a character- istic of O'Neill's playwriting. Now, however, there is no breaking of the play's realistic limits. When, for example, Mary is left alone at the end of the scene with Cathleen in Act Two, she speaks of her past in a long monologue that arises naturally from her addiction. As the morphine takes effect it causes her to babble, but she is still sufficiently aware not to be entirely dulled to her condition. Her words rise involuntarily out of her loneliness and guilt and speak of her longing for the life of the girl she was. It is as if she speaks to the girl in the past so as to assuage the loneliness of the present. Similarly, the long monologues of Edmund and his father in Act Four evoke the past as the only surcease from the doped present. Over their words there hangs no hint of Art Theatre Show Shop. O'Neill has enabled his actors to motivate the monologues and make them convincingly natural, psychologically real.

The two Tyrone plays hold firmly to the best realistic theatre practice. Yet for all their 'faithful realism', it should be remarked that the dramas more readily than many earlier works approach the abstraction and symbolism so characteristic of the expressionist mode. The quality and force of that abstraction is difficult to define. O'Neill does not try to convince his audiences that the world of the Tyrones is a microcosm, as he suggested with the typified chorus of *The Iceman Cometh*. The Tyrones and the Hogans are particular people, moving in a specific time, facing highly individual problems. Like many other works of the realistic American theatre – *Come Back, Little Sheba* or *A Hatful of Rain*, for example – the plays are contained and domestic, well-told case histories. Yet to call *Long*

Day's Journey Into Night a 'domestic tragedy' is to underestimate seriously its emotional effect. It is enlarged, not in the sense of Aristotelian 'heightening', but more by its unremitting movement 'behind life', in the phrase O'Neill once used to describe Strindberg's expressionist dramas. For a play to move 'behind life' means that it expands inward, through the surfaces, and toward the core of life itself. The inner enlargement of the Tyrone plays not only scrutinise the motives that produce the painful events, but somehow, also, they enlarge an audience's knowledge of the suffering these events produce. No drama of modern times contains more of pain's substance than *Long Day's Journey Into Night*, but in the final analysis, it is not the events, shocking through they are, that grip the audience. The Tyrones suffer and the spectators are convinced that, when suffering is the only reality, life is truly as it is depicted in the play.

Verisimilitude does not necessarily lead to a universal statement. However, when *Long Day's Journey Into Night* is played, another dimension opens. In the theatre, the suffering of the playwright is more real, if that is possible, than that of his characters. The audience shares them both, and moves as in a dream that is both real and more than real along the course of this 'Wander Play'. Pain exists in a double layer, one that can seem a fiction, one that must be a truth as the truth of suffering has seldom been stated. An emotion appropriate to an aesthetic experience and an emotion evoked by reality join to create in the spectators a capacity for pity that extends well beyond the boundaries of the theatre and rises to an acknowledgement of exceptional purity: that the universality of pain makes pity and understanding and forgiveness the greatest of human needs.

At their climactic moments, both the Tyrone plays convey the qualities of a dream. The fog or moonlight, the whiskey or dope causes the characters to drift in slow emotional movements. Activity ceases, and each play becomes 'a play for voices' that permits the lyrics of lamentation and loss to be heard clearly. Physical objects are only the source of reverie. Edmund and his father play cards. A bottle and glasses are on the table and above it an electric chandelier. Only these have substance in the room. The two men sit in near darkness and silence. A card is played or a drink is poured or a light bulb is turned on. Something in the outer world is touched, but it is a meaningless gesture. Then, as the object is touched, the mind recoils, moving away from that physical contact with the present into the past, wandering in a reverie that is as formless and far-reaching as the night outside. The reverie ended, the ballooning thought returns to the space where life is. Something else is touched;

reverie begins again, in a movement that is like a man's swimming, sinking and touching bottom in order to rise up again into the currents of the water. In such scenes, time as an adjunct of reality has stopped; forward motion has ended. The slow turning of memory is the play's only action. Life becomes a dream of pain.

What the morphine brings to the surface in Mary Tyrone is awareness of the isolation that is both her need and her terror. As she appears in the first scene of the play, although small hints of what is to follow quickly become apparent, she seems a woman to whom her home and family are all, as they were to Essie Miller in *Ah, Wilderness!* The dependence of the men on her is marked, and not only in their concern for her health. She emerges in the few moments of normality as the source of life for them, the quiet hub around which they move, happy in her presence. The summer house seems to be truly a home, and the comforts it offers, though modest, are sufficient to their well-being. The illusion of the home is an essential image to establish at the outset, for it, of course, is not what it seems. The room is shabby, poorly furnished, a temporary residence at best. It is like the cheap hotels of Tyrone's road tours, where Mary has waited alone, unable to associate with theatre people, spending nights in idleness until her husband comes or is brought home from the theatre. Mary's life has taught her loneliness and provided her with the definition of a home as a place where 'one is never lonely'. She remembers having had in her girlhood a 'real' home, yet the memory is illusory. Idealising her father, she has obliterated whatever faults existed in him. Tyrone tells Edmund her home was an ordinary one and her father a steady drinker. His implied question is whether Mary's girlhood was indeed the happy time she remembers it to have been. O'Neill makes clear that her desire, even as a girl, was to escape into a lonely world – into the convent where she could be sustained by a vision and live a simple, virginal existence. That Mary loves her husband admits no question, yet in a larger sense, love has disturbed her spirit and violated her desire to retain her encapsuled purity. Love has led her into a world for which she was not and never could be ready. She needs to be alone in a protected silence. She blames her failure vaguely on life, and she is right to do so. She says,

None of us can help the things life has done to us. They're done before you realise it, and once they're done they make you do other things until at last everything comes between you and what you'd like to be, and you've lost your true self forever.

In seeking her 'true self', Mary is looking for a self that does not exist. Repeatedly she remarks that she cannot find her glasses and therefore cannot see to fix her hair. In other words, she cannot see

what she is. She associates her Catholicism loosely with her need
for morphine. Morphine is medicine to still the pain in her arthritic
hands; the hands once played the piano; she studied music in the
convent. 'I had two dreams. To be a nun, that was the more
beautiful one. To become a concert pianist, that was the other.' But
the dreams of lost faith and spent talent are dreams of escape which
affect her as the morphine does by pulling her from the present,
from the house, from the irony of Tyrone's buying property without
providing a home, and from her indifference that is like hatred of
her family.

In the course of the play, Mary shifts repeatedly from a young
girl to a cynical embittered, self-contemptuous creature. Her guilt
at failing to take care of her dead child, Eugene, is translated into
insane hatred of her husband: 'I know why he wants to send you to
a sanatorium', she tells Edmund. 'To take you away from me! He's
always tried to do that. He's been jealous of every one of my babies!
He kept finding ways to make me leave them. That's what caused
Eugene's death. He's been jealous of you most of all. He knew I
loved you best because – ' Frantically babying Edmund does not
prevent her from blaming him for being born and starting her on
the dope habit. Edmund is her scourge and should never have been
born. Her hatred of Jamie is less ambiguous. Jamie's need for her is
by no means reciprocated. She hates his cynicism, turns from him
in fear that he will discover her need of the dope and silently accuses
him of murdering the dead child. When the morphine talks in her,
she treats her husband with a mixture of love and contempt, dwelling
on his failures and yet maintaining the truth of her love for him. As
Deborah Harford escaped in her dreams, Mary needs to turn from
them all, to find a path that will take her deep into the fog, hating
the loneliness, yet wanting to be rid of the obligations the men's
love place upon her. Edmund describes the blank wall she builds
around herself:

It's . . . like a bank of fog in which she hides and loses herself. Deliberately,
that's the hell of it! You know something in her does it deliberately – to get
beyond our reach, to be rid of us, to forget we're alive! It's as if, in spite of
loving us, she hated us!

Mary's refusal of all her responsibilities has bred in her a guilt
she is incapable of bearing. The morphine must be used to wipe out
'the pain – *all* the pain – I mean in my hands'. In the morphine
trance, she moves gently back in time, seeking to re-create the
illusions of a happier world, before there was a past to make her
what she has become. Her wedding dress, like Con Melody's red

uniform, is a symbol of something that never was a substantial reality. Her quest is for a hope lost, a goalless search for salvation never to be attained.

The men around Mary are condemned as she is to hopeless questing. Her husband like Con Melody is both poet and peasant. Under the graceful bearing of the aging actor, trained to eradicate the brogue, to gesture and speak with authority, there lies the fear of the poverty-stricken past. O'Neill has falsified to a degree the penny-pinching qualities in his father in drawing Tyrone, yet the fear his father felt was undoubtedly a real one, as was the sense he expressed of having failed his potential as an actor. Like Mary, Tyrone is doomed to an endless life of regret for something lost in the past, holding to a hope that has no reality. 'What the hell was it I wanted to buy?' he asks, and there is no answer unless it is protection and the quieting of irrational fears. His failure as an artist and as a husband had made him guilty beyond pardon. Like a lugged bear he stands as the target for all of his family's recriminations. Yet, perhaps more than any of the others, he shoulders the responsibilities of their lives. He has kindness in him, and a devotion to his wife that overrides all her animosity. For Edmund he demonstrates little close feeling. A generalised, somewhat distant affection is the most he reveals for his younger son. For Jamie, however, he has a strong feeling that is so positive it can turn easily into hostility. The two months during which Mary has returned to normal he describes to Jamie as 'heaven', and he adds, 'This home has been a home again. But I needn't tell you, Jamie.' O'Neill amplifies the sense of understanding with a stage direction:

His son looks at him, for the first time with an understanding sympathy. It is as if suddenly a deep bond of common feeling existed between them in which their antagonisms could be forgotten.

It is Jamie's sobbing in the final moments of the play that breaks Tyrone, and Jamie who evokes in him his only shows of violence and perhaps also his most bitter expression of sorrow. As his son lies drunk and unconscious he says with sadness,

A sweet spectacle for me! My first-born, who I hoped would bear my name in honor and dignity, who showed such brilliant promise!

Tyrone, more than any other member of the family, honors the bonds of the home. He is capable of love but is often driven toward hatred. Even so, he never truly hates, but lives isolated within the frame of the bond, attempting to love in spite of everything. He turns from the pain of his life, to the local bar-room; he buys bad real estate to purchase security he cannot find; he drinks to dope his mind to the point of forgetfulness. But he does not betray. He remains a simple man, free of cynicism, incapable of hatred. O'Neill's view of his father contains full charity.

O'Neill's picture of his younger self and of his brother Jamie is on the surface clear enough. Jamie, like his brother and father, is lost, embittered and cynical, wanting his mother whose rejection of him perhaps reaches farther back than the time when morphine forced her into drugged isolation. To compensate for her loss, he has sought to destroy himself with the profligate life of the Broadway rounder, and he has attempted to corrupt his brother, in the pretence of 'putting him wise' to women and liquor. In Jamie, pain can have no anodyne. Liquor, far from dulling his loss, makes it unbearable, and, while Edmund is fussed over, even babied, no one tries to help Jamie. Nor is escape possible. Edmund can move into the fog – as he does in the third act – and find a kind of peace. The peace of belonging to a secret at the source of life, 'the vision of beatitude' which he attempts to describe to his father, offers him a way out, just as Mary's dream of finding her girlhood faith and Tyrone's memory of Booth's praise have power to assuage the present. There is no vision of beatitude for Jamie in *Long Day's Journey Into Night*. His need is always beside him, in Mary, but he cannot reach her. Like Tantalus, he has no refuge from desire. His is the howl of a soul lost in hell.

Edmund, as O'Neill presents him, is clearly drawn, and, as a dramatic character, offers adequate material to an actor, but there is perhaps less truth in his portrait than in the others. He is a strangely neutral figure, except in the scene with his father in Act Four. Even there he speaks out of a solitude that is unlike the isolation of the others. Although O'Neill has been at pains to show what the past has made his parents and brother, it is unclear what the past has made Edmund. O'Neill perhaps understandably suppresses the fact of his brief marriage and his child and omits the crucial event in 1912 of his divorce. He mentions that Edmund has been to sea, and almost perfunctorily adds that he has lived in the sewers of New York and Buenos Aires and has attempted suicide. None of these events, except in so far as his having been to sea conditions his vision of belonging, bear heavily on what he is. He seems to be the victim of the family, unwanted, betrayed, led astray by his brother and, now, with tuberculosis, suffering under his father's penuriousness. It is easy – perhaps too easy – to sympathise with Edmund. He is no more than an embittered adolescent, certainly a pale copy of what Eugene O'Neill was at that time. . . .

SOURCE: extract from chapter ('The Door and the Mirror') in *Contour in Time: The Plays of Eugene O'Neill* (New York and London, 1972), pp. 422, 425–32.

Judith E. Barlow   'Edmund in the Final Act'   (1985)

. . . O'Neill designed the play very carefully so that Edmund hears the other characters' accounts of how they erred. He is on-stage for all of the final act except the opening moments. He hears his brother and father tell how forces around them and their own blunders destroyed them, and he is warned. He is warned by Mary much earlier. In the second act's final scene, Mary tells him that some day she will be cured, 'some day when the Blessed Virgin Mary forgives me and gives me back the faith in Her love and pity I used to have in my convent days, and I can pray to Her again – '. These words show that Mary will not even try to help herself; she will merely wait passively for the Virgin's aid. In the notes O'Neill indicates his intention to move this speech to the very end of the play and, in fact, the final speech in the scenario is very similar to this. O'Neill wisely chose not to conclude *Journey* with this passage for several reasons: it focuses too sharply on Mary rather than on the family as a whole; it shows Mary aware of her present problem, an awareness she has lost well before the last scene of the published text; and it is a much less dramatic ending than the one he ultimately composed. O'Neill probably also left the speech in the second act because he wanted to emphasise that Edmund hears what his mother says. Edmund is alone with her here (as he is not at the play's conclusion) and he is neither drunk nor exhausted. Edmund does hear Mary, and what she is saying is that she will not, or cannot, attempt to help herself. The situation is beyond her control, and beyond Edmund's.

In the last act Edmund listens to Tyrone's tale about how he was ruined by the 'big money maker' he starred in too long. After this speech Edmund tells his father, 'I know you a lot better now'. The emphatic 'a lot' was added to the typescript. He then, under protest, hears Jamie's confession, which ends with the admonition: 'Only don't forget me. Remember I warned you – for your sake.' Edmund has already shown that he knows the value of remembering. Early in the play he exhorts his mother to recall her previous drug episodes and warns: 'it's bad for you to forget. The right way is to remember. So you'll always be on your guard.' This is the advice Edmund must follow: to remember what Mary, Tyrone and Jamie have told him.

The manuscript includes one curious scene absent from subsequent drafts, an appearance by Mary roughly one-quarter of the way into the final act. In the published text Edmund at this point fears 'she's coming downstairs', but she retreats without being seen by the audience. There are likely many reasons why O'Neill deleted this scene; the simplest explanation is that it serves virtually no purpose. Mary wanders about looking for 'something I lost long ago – something I miss dreadfully now' and concludes 'I could never find it here'. These lines are confusing as well as unnecessary because, despite a reference by Mary to the convent, they might mislead the audience into believing that the object of her search is the wedding gown with which she appears at the drama's climax. What Mary seeks cannot be found in the attic any more than in the living room: it is her lost faith and childhood innocence. Further, this scene detracts from the stunning impact of the play's final moments when Mary, who has been absent from the stage for an hour, enters dramatically in a blaze of light. O'Neill's theatrical sense alone might have impelled him to eliminate the earlier appearance. Finally, surely one reason O'Neill cancelled Mary's premature entrance was to keep the audience's attention on Edmund. Up until the final act Mary dominates the play; during the first three acts of the published text she speaks more lines than do all the men combined. She is the dramatic focus of *Journey*, just as Hickey is the dramatic focus of *Iceman*. Deleting Mary's appearance at this point removes a distraction from Edmund's learning experience. He has already learned, in previous scenes, all that his mother's situation can teach him.

Like Larry Slade in *Iceman*, Edmund Tyrone learns the necessity for pity. Both characters are forced to listen to confessions they do not want to hear, and both are compelled to temper their cynicism with compassionate understanding. Edmund does try to quell fights throughout the play, but it is especially in the fourth act that he functions as peace-maker. When Tyrone and Jamie start to battle just before the final scene, Edmund refuses to join Jamie's attack on their father and attempts to squelch the argument. In the scenario, by contrast, Edmund's feelings for his father at this point are more equivocal. Although he is immediately ashamed of his words and tries to cover them with appeasing statements, Edmund's vicious attack on the old man – his claim that Tyrone likes to have a failure around so he can feel superior – occurs here. His anger has not been fully assuaged by the family's revelations. Shortly thereafter, in all drafts, Edmund defends Mary from Jamie's nasty tongue. In the scenario he orders his brother, 'Stop it, damn you! Leave her alone', when Jamie cries 'All hopped up. Our mother' and 'mockingly' recites Kipling's 'Mother o' Mine'. His reaction is surer and swifter in the published text: he strikes his brother for his cruel comparison of Mary to Ophelia.

Even more than Larry Slade, however, Edmund is a character whose importance is difficult to convey on stage. He functions as the audience's touchstone: our perceptions grow as his do. The very structure of *Journey* forces us into a position analogous to Edmund's: he knew something was wrong with his mother long before he discovered the exact nature of her malady, just as we must wait through one and a half acts before her addiction is revealed to us. Like Edmund, we are witness to the wrenching confessions of the other Tyrones. Yet Edmund's sympathetic responses are relatively minor: he is never required to act as decisively on his newly acquired understanding and forgiveness as Larry is. His compassionate deeds – telling his father he knows him 'a lot better now', intervening in family fights, protecting Tyrone and Mary from Jamie's verbal assaults – are small ones. Larry, on the other hand, must undertake a shattering dramatic action: the condemnation of Parritt. Jamie thanks Edmund for listening to his confession as Parritt thanks Larry for listening to and acting upon his. But it is Jamie himself who makes the greater sacrifice, who gives up his cherished self-image as his brother's protector to warn his brother that there is hatred in him as well as love.

When José Quintero first presented *Long Day's Journey Into Night* in November 1956, he asked Jason Robards Jnr, who had made such a success as Hickey in the *Iceman* revival, to play the role of Edmund. Even though Edmund is the larger part (he is on stage longer and speaks more lines than his brother), Robards requested to play Jamie instead. Reviewers of that production consistently praised the portrayal of the elder brother. Henry Hewes, among others, claimed that Robards stole the show. Equally consistently critics complained that Edmund is a less interesting character than his parents and brother, and gave more attention to the other roles. It does not appear to be the performance of Bradford Dillman (who played Edmund in the original production) that is responsible for this judgement, since his acting was often praised. Walter Kerr, for example, contended that Dillman handled his speeches 'with swift, sensitive skill', yet he accorded Edmund and Dillman only half a sentence while spending three paragraphs discussing the other Tyrones and the actors and actress portraying them. [See Kerr's review in section 2 of this Part Three, above – Ed.] In reviews of the movie version and of revivals, critics continued to complain about the paleness of the younger son. An anonymous *Time* reviewer, commenting on the movie, echoed many critics when he concluded that Edmund is 'the 'weakest of the parts'.

We have seen how much care O'Neill gave to the portrayal of Edmund, and how alterations in the various drafts help to focus attention on him as a unique and important figure. But despite the effort expended on Edmund's characterisation he is, on stage, less compelling than the others. One clue may be found in the crucial last-act speeches. Tyrone's and Jamie's confessions are very personal, emotionally devastating admissions of failure. While Edmund's sea speech is moving, there is little of the pathos of personal pain and failure in it. One is as struck by the way he describes his sea experiences as by the experiences themselves. Almost a set piece on the miseries of any sensitive soul, it is not drawn from the torments of individual defeat as are the words of his father and brother, and his mother's anguished ravings. Nothing in the logic of the play demands that Edmund should have erred and suffered the same way the rest of the Tyrones have, but the fact that he has not makes him a less emotionally affecting character.

The other problems are very similar to those O'Neill faced with *Iceman*. As Larry Slade must compete on stage with the flamboyant Hickey and Harry Hope, so Edmund must compete for attention with two actors and a dope-crazed Mary. By the very nature of the character O'Neill has created, Edmund is less colorful and dynamic than the other family members. He is the quiet one. This contrast is further heightened because much of Edmund's function, like Larry's, is to listen and learn – basically passive, undramatic activities. It is only in his last play that O'Neill creates a character, Josie Hogan in *A Moon for the Misbegotten*, who as sympathetic listener is as dramatically compelling as those with a tale of suffering to tell. . . .

SOURCE: extract from chapter on the play in *Final Acts* (Athens, Georgia, 1985), pp. 108–11.

168

Jean Chothia   The Final Scene's Mysterious
Effectiveness   (1979)

... the ending of *Mourning Becomes Electra* was one of the most convincing signs of the imaginative control which O'Neill would achieve in the late plays. It was in many ways a tour de force imposing order on the play. The unfolding action of *Long Day's Journey Into Night* has a greater coherence and the dialogue is more absorbingly complex than that of the earlier play. The ending, when it arrives, comes as the culmination of the meanings, and undertones and overtones we have absorbed during the play, and it is couched in words and images made potent by their use within the play. In [discussing] the language of the play, it is important to look at the final sequence which, in its quiet and stillness, is so different from that of *The Iceman Cometh*. The sequence has been praised repeatedly: the method of this study should enable us to put into words some, at least, of the reasons for its extraordinary power.

O'Neill altered Act Four in its second draft to keep Mary offstage until the last few minutes of the play. In doing so, he increased the suspense of the act and the subsequent impact of Mary's appearance. Throughout the act her entrance is anticipated, by the listening attitude of the men, by their comments on her restless pacing above them and by their very presence on the stage, since we recognise that their vigil must continue until she has become still. If we catch it, the reference to Ibsen's *John Gabriel Borkman* is an appropriate one with its memory of that other familial relationship, its tortured, listening women and its intimacy and destructiveness. The underlying pattern of the action demands Mary's presence for its completion. Edmund and Tyrone have moved three times from hostility to understanding, reaching a deeper level of mutual confidence at each stage. Then, the relationship between the two brothers has been presented with comparable intensification as Jamie has moved from bonhomie to threat, to self-revelation. Each of the three men having in turn exposed his secret thought to one of the others, there is a hiatus. Exhausted, they drowse. The balance in which the characters have been held until now makes Mary's entrance inevitable. But it is also startling because of the way in which it takes place. There is a moment of silence and then Edmund jerks up, listening intently. A burst of light at the back of the stage, when all five bulbs of the chandelier flash on, is followed by a burst of sound, when a Chopin waltz is played on the piano. When Mary appears in the doorway, her hair is long and braided girlishly, she wears a sky blue night gown and carries a wedding dress. O'Neill succeeds in creating a poetry of theatre here where he failed in *Dynamo*, for all the elaborate machinery of that play, because each visual and aural impression arouses in the audience some memory of the dialogue. Things which through repeated naming have become emblems of the private mythology of the family are suddenly present before us in solid form. Jamie's words, which break the silence, have the force of words which should not have been spoken but, having been, cannot be expunged from the mind and Mary's failure to react to them signifies how dissociated from the present she has become. When she speaks she uses the schoolgirlish register entirely, 'I play *so* badly now. I'm *all* out of practice. Sister Theresa will give me a *dreadful* scolding . . .' She is no longer speaking in the present and looking back to the past but, as the verb tenses show, has moved into that past time which has become her present. There follows the highly patterned passage containing the poem after which Mary speaks her final monologue.

Here, as throughout the play, the verbal and visual level are integrated with each other, so that, when words leave off, the stage image speaks. Once we have absorbed the impact of Mary's final entrance, the stage picture has significance not because, like that, it is startling or spectacular, but because of the way it complements the dialogue. Watching the final moments of the play, we are scarcely aware of how carefully movement and gesture have been organised and how much they contribute to the feeling of the scene. . . . The men remain still so that our eyes follow Mary as she crosses from the door to the front of the stage. Mary's seemingly aimless movement, in fact, takes her past each of the men in turn, taking our attention with her from one to the other of them. In the single other movement, shortly after Mary's entrance, Tyrone approaches Mary who carries her wedding dress that has lain in the old trunk in the attic and that, described with delight by Mary earlier in the play, had become an emblem of her lost girlhood and her reproach to Tyrone. Because we have experienced this, Tyrone's simple gesture of taking the dress from her and holding it protectively is remarkably moving. When Mary comes to rest it is . . . at the front left corner of the stage which leaves the silent characters at the focal point in the centre. This divides the audience's attention during Mary's final speech and so acts as preparation for the last line of the play.

Whilst Mary speaks her monologue, the audience, listening to her words, observe the speaking silence of the listening men and hear, perhaps, the lingering echo of the poem, 'There is no help for all these things are so'. They recognise that Mary has given herself over to the past, obliterating her men-folk with her colloquialisms, her girlish intensifiers, her manner of discussing the interview as if it had just taken place. Her naïve and trusting words, 'I knew She heard my prayer and would always love me and see no harm ever came to me as long as I never lost my faith in her', are almost unbearable for the stage listeners, and for the audience observing the stage listeners and knowing that their perspective is from a different point in time from hers.

The overwhelming effect of the last four lines of the play comes, I think, because, just when it appears that the play has drawn to its conclusion and has reached some kind of resting place, however dismal, the sentence, '*That was* in the winter of senior year', pushes the interview back into the distant past and returns Mary to the present and the family, from which there can be, after all, no escape for any of the four Tyrones. The quiet ending of the play is not a conclusion but another relentless beginning:

That was in the winter of senior year. Then in the spring something happened to me. Yes, I remember. I fell in love with James Tyrone and was so happy for a time.

SOURCE: extract from chapter on the play in *Forging a Language* (Cambridge, 1979), pp. 181–4.

Timo Tiusanen   'Dynamic Realism'   (1968)

. . . According to certain formulas of critical thought, *Long Day's Journey Into Night* should be a poor play. It is 'undoubtedly too long – one long scene seems almost irrelevant; there is too much quoting of classic poetry; and the deliberate formlessness of it all is enervating. Still, it is a dramatic achievement of the first order,' 'a master-piece'.[1] . . .

If a play is a masterpiece 'in spite of' several critical presupposi-tions, it is high time to start asking whether there is anything wrong – with the presuppositions. If we have not given up the hope of finding rational explanations to art, we should be busy looking for reasons *why Long Day's Journey Into Night* is a masterpiece – instead of weighing down the other end of the scale with our inapplicable criteria. One thing is certain: emotional power does not come through on the stage without some kind of technique; only physical power might. And *Long Day's Journey Into Night* does not shout; it speaks through its form.

Admitting that the play is void of outer action, there is good reason to emphasise that it is full of inner action. It is within the speeches that a major part of the drama is acted; it is within the utterances that the masks are changed. O'Neill let himself be bound by the tradition of realism because he knew that he could utilise the amount of freedom granted to him by the shortish chain of this style. He was convinced of his ability to dance in these chains. He knew that he could write in a style infiltrated by the results of his experimental period; he knew how to achieve porousness by making every detail both realistic and symbolic. 'His contrapuntal arrangement of events that are seen in the theatre and reported events, which become real in the theatre of the mind only, makes his realism a free and spacious style', Stamm writes,[2] recognising clearly an important aspect of O'Neill dynamic realism. Yet the reminiscent speeches of *Long Day's Journey Into Night* would be static if O'Neill had not employed his small circles, drawn to touch love and hatred, sympathy and antagonism, guilt and accusations. O'Neill does not only move backwards in time, he also makes the past present. The past is an actual phenomenon, not asking but demanding reactions from the agonised characters. The wild fluctuation in the mind of Caligula or Ponce de Leon was attached only to the stage situation; now O'Neill has also the rich orchestra of human memories to play with.

'The past is the present, isn't it? It's the future, too. We all try to lie out of that but life won't let us', Mary complains in one of her most lucid moments. If the first sentence could be taken as the motto for O'Neill's technique, the second reveals the core of his tragic vision. In fact, this is a statement in which O'Neill's method of constructing his play and his vision meet one another. The circle had been his favorite structural formula ever since his early efforts: yet as late as in this confessional play we see how deeply it was rooted in his personal attitude toward life. Fate is in the circles, in the inescapable repetitions, in the power of the past over the present and over the future. It may shout with the foghorn, too – but the sound has a meaning only to those who are living through the long chain of small, inescapable circles. This is O'Neill's modern artistic approximation to Fate, more personal than his psychological one in *Mourning Becomes Electra*.

The basic motivation for the numerous repetitions in *Long Day's*

Journey Into Night is given above. Facing the paradox of length once again, we might formulate a question: how many links can one take out of a chain and still make it reach? The more links that are added to a chain, the longer and weightier it becomes; and to those who prefer chains of a smaller calibre, all that can be said is that these are the shackles given to his characters by a tragedian. Some of the repetitions are further motivated by an urge to render ironically conflicting versions of familiar stories at different points of the action and by different characters: Tyrone's picture of Mary's father deviates from that cherished by Mary herself; Mary speaks of her falling in love in contrasting ways. If after these considerations there is still a temptation to abridge, let it happen in small bits, mostly somewhere in the first three acts. It certainly will not do to say in an off-hand manner that 'there is too much quoting of classic poetry' or that a whole scene is irrelevant.

Long Day's Journey Into Night is seen by Mottram as a synthesis of O'Neill's playwriting career. His 'earliest one-acters melt into Edmund's sea-voyaging region of dream reality'; there is material from the saloons, utilised even in a group of other plays; *The Straw* is represented by Edmund's tuberculosis; 'the Strindbergian elemental family is at last achieved without bogus classicism or pop-Freudianism'; and 'the calm of *The Iceman Cometh* comes through again in this last harbour'.[3] It is possible to speak of a synthesis from another point of view as well: O'Neill applies here several scenic means of expression he knows thoroughly from previous usages. There is the idea of the fog, expressed mainly through a repetitive sound effect; there are modified monologues, again as the climaxes of the play; there is a continuous circular movement in the dialogue; symbolic significance gradually gathers around one portion of the setting; there are quotations rendering an additional layer of meaning. In a way, the quotations are still another modification of masks: by reciting a poem it is possible for the characters to express feelings not otherwise revealed.

All these means of expression are used in a purposeful way and executed flawlessly within the limits of the style chosen by the playwright: dynamic realism. Even in a play with little or no plot there can be quite a lot of interaction between the scenic images. Besides, Long Day's Journey Into Night has a plot of an unconventional kind: its action proceeds through the fog into the monologues. Agreeing with Gassner in that 'a continuing tension between naturalism and a variety of alternatives of dramatic stylisation has characterised the century's theatre',[4] we might call Long Day's Journey Into Night one of O'Neill's major answers to the challenge created by this tension. It is more than a major answer: it is a masterful one.

SOURCE: extract from chapter ('Through Fog to Monologue') in *O'Neill's Scenic Images* (Princeton, N.J., 1968), pp. 300–3.

NOTES

[Reorganised and renumbered from the original – Ed.]

1. Croswell Bowen, *The Curse of the Misbegotten* (New York, 1959), pp. 273, 366.
2. Rudolph Stamm, '"Faithful Realism": Eugene O'Neill and the Problem of Style', *English Studies*, 40, 4 (Aug. 1959), p. 249.
3. Eric Mottram, 'Men and Gods: A Study of Eugene O'Neill', *Encore*, 105 (Sept.–Oct. 1963), p. 43.
4. John Gassner, *Theatre at the Crossroads* (New York, 1960), p. *xiv*.

Robert Brustein 'The Journey into the Past' (1962)

. . . There is a curse on the blighted house of the Tyrones, and the origin of the curse lies elsewhere, with existence itself. As Mary says: 'None of us can help the things life has done to us.' In tracing down the origin of this curse, O'Neill has returned to the year 1912; but as the play proceeds, he brings us even further into the past. Implicated in the misfortunes of the house are not only the two generations of Tyrones, but a previous generation as well; Edmund's attempted suicide, before the action begins, is linked to the suicide of Tyrone's father, and Edmund's consumption is the disease by which Mary's father died. Though O'Neill does not mention this, the tained legacy reaches into the future, too: the playwright's elder son, Eugene Jnr, is also to commit suicide, and his younger son, Shane, is to become, like his grandmother, a narcotics addict. The generations merge, and so does Time. 'The past is the present, isn't it?' cries Mary. 'It's the future too. We all try to lie out of that but life won't let us.'

O'Neill, the probing artist, seeks in the past for the origination of guilt and blame; but his characters seek happiness and dreams. All four Tyrones share an intense hatred of the present and its morbid, inescapable reality. All four seek solace from the shocks of life in nostalgic memories, which they reach through different paths. For

Mary, the key that turns the lock of the past is morphine. 'It kills the pain. You go back until at last you are beyond its reach. Only the past when you were happy is real.' The pain she speaks of is in her crippled hands, the constant reminder of her failed dream to be a concert pianist, but even more it is in her crippled, guilty soul. Mary has betrayed all her hopes and dreams. Even her marriage is a betrayal, since she longed to be a nun, wholly dedicated to her namesake, the Blessed Virgin; but her addiction betrays her religion, family and home. She cannot pray; she is in a state of despair; and the accusations of her family only aggravate her guilt. Mary is subject to a number of illusions – among them, the belief that she married beneath her – but unlike the derelicts of *The Iceman*, who dream of the future, she only dreams of the past. Throughout the action, she is trying to escape the pain of the present entirely; and at the end, with the aid of drugs, she has finally returned to the purity, innocence and hope of her girlhood. Although the title of the play suggests a progress, therefore, the work moves always backwards. The long journey is a journey into the past.

O'Neill suggests this in many ways, partly through ambiguous images of light and dark, sun and mist. The play begins at 8:30 in the morning with a trace of fog in the air, and concludes sometime after midnight, with the house fogbound – the mood changing from sunny cheer over Mary's apparent recovery to gloomy despair over her new descent into hell. The night-time scenes occur logically at the end of the day; but subjectively, the night precedes the day, for the play closes on a phantasmagoria of past time. Under the influence of Mary's drugs – and, to some extent, the alcohol of the men – time evaporates and hovers, and disappears: past, present, future become one. Mary drifts blissfully into illusions under cover of the night, which functions like a shroud against the harsh, daylight reality. And so does that fog that Mary loves: 'It hides you from the world and the world from you', she says. 'You feel that everything has changed, and nothing is what it seemed to be. No one can find or touch you any more.' Her love for her husband and children neutralised by her terrible sense of guilt, Mary withdraws more and more into herself. And this, in turn, intensifies the unhappiness of the men: 'The hardest thing to take', says Edmund, 'is the black wall she builds around herself. Or it's more like a bank of fog in which she hides and loses herself. . . . It's as if, in spite of loving us, she hated us.'

Mary, however, is not alone among the 'fog people' – the three men also have their reasons for withdrawing into night. Although less shrouded in illusion than Mary, each, nevertheless, haunts the past like a ghost, seeking consolation for a wasted life. For Tyrone, his youth was a period of artistic promise when he had the potential to be a great actor instead of a commercial hack; his favorite memory is of Booth's praising his Othello, words which he has written down and lost. For Jamie, who might have borne the Tyrone name 'in honor and dignity, who showed such brilliant promise', the present is without possibility; he is now a hopeless ne'er-do-well, pursuing oblivion in drink and the arms of fat whores while mocking his own failure in bathetic, self-hating accents: 'My name is Might-Have-Been', he remarks, quoting from Rossetti; 'I am also called No More, Too Late, Farewell.' For Edmund, who is more like his mother than the others, night and fog are a refuge from the curse of living:

The fog was where I wanted to be. . . . That's what I wanted – to be alone with myself in another world where truth is untrue and life can hide from itself. . . . It was like walking on the bottom of the sea. As if I had drowned long ago. As if I was a ghost belonging to the fog, and the fog was the ghost of the sea. It felt damned peaceful to be nothing more than a ghost within a ghost.

Reality, truth, and life plague him like a disease. Ashamed of being human, he finds existence itself detestable: 'Who wants to see life as it is, if they can help it? It's the three Gorgons in one. You look in their faces and die. Or it's Pan. You see him and die – that is, inside you – and have to go on living as a ghost.'

'We are such stuff as manure is made on, so let's drink up and forget it' – like Strindberg, who developed a similar excremental view of humankind, the young Edmund has elected to withdraw from Time by whatever means available, and one of these is alcohol. Edmund, whose taste in poetry is usually execrable, finally quotes a good poet, Baudelaire, on the subject of drunkenness: 'Be drunken, if you would not be martyred slaves of Time; be drunken continually! With wine, with poetry, or with virtue, as you will.' And in order to avoid being enslaved by Time, Edmund contemplates other forms of drunkenness as well. In his fine fourth-act speech, he tells of his experiences at sea, when he discovered Nirvana for a moment, pulling out of Time and dissolving into the infinite:

I belonged, without past or future, within peace and unity and a wild joy, within something greater than my own life, or the life of Man, to Life itself! To God, if you want to put it that way. . . . For a second you see – and seeing the secret, are the secret. For a second there is meaning! Then the hand lets the veil fall and you are alone, lost in the fog again, and you stumble on towards nowhere, for no good reason.

The ecstatic vision of wholeness is only momentary, and Edmund, who 'would have been more successful as a sea-gull or a fish', must once again endure the melancholy fate of living in reality: 'As it is, I will always be a stranger who never feels at home, who does not really want and is not really wanted, who can never belong, who must always be a little in love with death!' In love with death since death is the ultimate escape from Time, the total descent into night and fog.

There is a fifth Tyrone involved in the play – the older Eugene O'Neill. And although he has superimposed his later on his earlier self (Edmund, described as a socialist and atheist, has many religious-existential attitudes), the author and the character are really separable. Edmund wishes to deny Time, but O'Neill has elected to return to it once again – reliving the past and mingling with his ghosts – in order to find the secret and meaning of their suffering. For the playwright has discovered another escape besides alcohol, Nirvana, or death from the terrible chaos of life: the escape of art where chaos is ordered and the meaningless made meaningful. The play itself is an act of forgiveness and reconciliation, the artist's life-long resentment disintegrated through complete understanding of the past and total self-honesty.

These qualities dominate the last act, which proceeds through a sequence of confessions and revelations to a harrowing climax. Structurally, the act consists of two long colloquies – the first between Tyrone and Edmund, the second between Edmund and Jamie – followed by a long soliloquy from Mary who, indeed, concludes every act. Tyrone's confession of failure as an actor finally makes him understandable to Edmund who thereupon forgives him all his faults; and Jamie's confession of his ambivalent feelings towards his brother, and his half-conscious desire to make him fail too, is the deepest psychological moment in the play. But the most honest moment of self-revelation occurs at the end of Edmund's speech, after he has tried to explain the origin of his bitterness and despair. Tyrone, as usual, finds his son's musing 'morbid', but he has to admit that Edmund has 'the makings of a poet'. Edmund replies:

The *makings* of a poet. No, I'm afraid I'm like the guy who is always panhandling for a smoke. He hasn't even got the makings. He's got only the habit. I couldn't touch what I tried to tell you just now. I just stammered. That's the best I'll ever do. . . . Well, it will be faithful realism, at least. Stammering is the native eloquence of us fog people.

In describing his own limitations as a dramatist, O'Neill here rises to real eloquence; speaking the truth has given him a tongue. Having accepted these limitations, and dedicated himself to a 'faithful realism' seen through the lens of the 'family kodak', he has turned into a dramatist of the very first rank.

Mary's last speech is the triumph of his new dramatic method, poetically evoking all the themes of the play; and it is marvellously prepared for. The men are drunk, sleepy and exhausted after all the wrangling; the lights are very low; the night and fog very thick. Suddenly, a *coup de théâtre*. All the bulbs in the front parlor chandelier are illuminated, and the opening bars of a Chopin waltz are haltingly played, 'as if an awkward schoolgirl were practising it for the first time'. The men are shocked into consciousness as Mary enters, absent-mindedly trailing her wedding dress. She is so completely in the past that even her features have been transfigured: 'the uncanny thing is that her face now appears so youthful'. What follows is a scene remarkably like Lady Macbeth's sleepwalking scene, or, as Jamie cruelly suggests, Ophelia's mad scene – an audaciously theatrical and, at the same time, profoundly moving expression from the depths of a tormented soul.

While the men look on in horror, Mary re-enacts the dreams of her youth, oblivious of her surroundings; and her speeches sum up the utter hopelessness of the entire family. Shy and polite, like a young schoolgirl, astonished at her swollen hands and at the elderly gentleman who gently takes the wedding dress from her grasp, Mary is back in the convent, preparing to become a nun. She is looking for something, 'something I need terribly', something that protected her from loneliness and fear: 'I can't have lost it forever. I would die if I thought that. Because then there would be no hope.' It is her life, and, even more, her faith. She has had a vision of the Blessed Virgin, who had 'smiled and blessed me with her consent'. But the Mother Superior has asked her to live like other girls before deciding to take her vows, and she reluctantly has agreed:

I said, of course, I would do anything she suggested, but I knew it was simply a waste of time. After I left her, I felt all mixed up, so I went to the shrine and prayed to the Blessed Virgin and found peace again because I knew she heard my prayer and would always love me and see no harm ever came to me so long as I never lost my faith in her.

But the faith has turned yellow, like her wedding dress, and harm has indeed come. On the threshold of the later horror, Mary grows uneasy; then puts one foot over into the vacancy which is to come: 'That was in the winter of senior year. Then in the springtime something happened to me. Yes, I remember. I fell in love with James Tyrone and was so happy for a time.'

Her mournful speech, which concludes on the key word of the play, spans the years and breaks them, recapitulating all the blighted hopes, the persistent illusions, the emotional ambivalence, and the sense of imprisonment in the fate of others that the family shares. It leaves the central character enveloped in fog, and the others encased in misery, the night deepening around their shameful secrets. But it signalises O'Neill's journey out of the night and into the daylight – into a perception of his true role as a man and an artist – exorcising his ghosts and 'facing my dead at last'. . . .

SOURCE: extract from chapter on O'Neill in *The Theatre of Revolt* (Boston, Mass., 1962), pp. 352–8.

SELECT BIBLIOGRAPHY

EDITIONS

The following are the play-text editions most readily available in paperback:

For *Mourning Becomes Electra* – Eugene O'Neill, *Three Plays* (Vintage Books, New York, 1959); and Eugene O'Neill, *Mourning Becomes Electra* (Cape, London, 1966).

For *Iceman* – Eugene O'Neill, *The Iceman Cometh* (Vintage Books, New York, 1957; Cape, London, 1966).

For *Long Day's Journey* – Eugene O'Neill, *Long Day's Journey Into Night* (Yale University Press, 1956; Cape, London, 1966).

The best standard edition of O'Neill's works is *Eugene O'Neill: The Complete Plays*, published in three volumes in 1988 by The Library of America, New York.

BIBLIOGRAPHY AND CONCORDANCE

The most complete bibliography of the plays is to be found in Jennifer McCabe Atkinson, *Eugene O'Neill: A Descriptive Bibliography* (University of Pittsburgh Press, 1974).

Oscar Cargill, N. Bryllion Fagin and William J. Fisher (eds) in their *O'Neill and His Plays* (New York University Press, 1961) provide a fine selected bibliography and an excellent source-book, containing material by and about O'Neill.

A complete listing of all publication dates and major productions, excerpts from reviews of original performances and revivals, and a full (USA) bibliography up to 1972, can be found in Jordan Y. Miller, *Eugene O'Neill and the American Critics* (Archon Books, Hampden, Conn., 1973).

A complete concordance of the plays has been compiled by J. Russell Reaver in *An O'Neill Concordance* (Gale Research Co., Detroit, 1969).

ANTHOLOGIES OF CRITICISM

Seven very good selections of O'Neill criticism are:

Harold Bloom (ed.), *Eugene O'Neill's 'The Iceman Cometh'* (Chelsea House, New York, 1987);

Virginia Floyd (ed.), *Eugene O'Neill: A World View* (Frederick Ungar, New York, 1979);

John Gassner (ed.), *O'Neill: A Collection of Critical Essays* (Prentice-Hall, Englewood Cliffs, N.J., 1964);

Ernest G. Griffin (ed.), *Eugene O'Neill: A Collection of Criticism* (McGraw-Hill, New York, 1976);

Jordan Y. Miller (ed.), *Playwright's Progress: O'Neill and the Critics* (Scott Foresman, Chicago, 1965);

John Henry Raleigh (ed.), *'The Iceman Cometh': A Collection of Critical Essays* – in the 'Twentieth-Century Interpretations' series (Prentice-Hall, Englewood Cliffs, N.J., 1968);

John H. Stroupe (ed.), *Critical Approaches to O'Neill* (AMS Press, New York, 1988).

BIOGRAPHY

The two best biographies of O'Neill are:
Arthur and Barbara Gelb, *O'Neill* (Harper and Row, New York, 1962);
Louis Sheaffer, *O'Neill: Son and Playwright* and *O'Neill: Son and Artist* (Little, Brown, Boston, 1968 and 1973 respectively).

GENERAL AND PARTICULAR STUDIES

Valuable books on the dramatist and his work, additional to those represented in this Casebook, are:
Doris Alexander, *The Tempering of Eugene O'Neill* (New York, 1962);
Leonard Chabrowe, *Ritual and Pathos: The Theater of O'Neill* (Lewisburg, Pa., 1976);
Barrett Clark, *Eugene O'Neill: The Man and His Plays* (New York, 1947);
Peter Egri, *Chekhov and O'Neill* (Budapest, 1986);
Edwin A. Engel, *The Haunted Heroes of Eugene O'Neill* (Cambridge, Mass., 1953);
Doris V. Falk, *Eugene O'Neill and the Tragic Tension* (New Brunswick, N.J., 1958);
Virginia Floyd, *The Plays of Eugene O'Neill* (New York, 1985);
Winifred D. Frazer, *Love as Death in 'The Iceman Cometh'* (Gainesville, Fla., 1967);
John Gassner, *Eugene O'Neill* (Minneapolis, 1965);
Clifford Leech, *Eugene O'Neill* (New York, 1963);
John Orlandello, *O'Neill on Film* (Rutherford, N.J., 1982);
James A Robinson, *Eugene O'Neill and Oriental Thought* (Carbondale, Ill., 1983);
Robert K. Sarlos, *Jig Cook and the Provincetown Players: Theatre in Ferment* (Amherst, Mass., 1982);
Richard Dana Skinner, *Eugene O'Neill: A Poet's Quest* (New York, 1964);
Gary Vena, *Eugene O'Neill's 'The Iceman Cometh': A Reconstruction of the 1946 Theatre Guild Production* (Ann Arbor, Mich., 1987).

NOTES ON CONTRIBUTORS

BROOKS ATKINSON (1894–1984): distinguished drama critic for the *New York Times* and author of many books on theatre, including *Broadway* (1970).

JUDITH BARLOW: Associate Professor of English in the State University of New York at Albany; her work on American drama includes *Final Acts: The Creation of Three Late O'Neill Plays* (1986).

ROBERT BENCHLEY (1880–1945): American humorist and an influential drama critic (for *Life* magazine and *New Yorker*).

ERIC BENTLEY: noted translator of Brecht and Pirandello and writer of several plays, this British-born American critic has taught at Columbia University and at the State University of New York. His works on drama and theatre criticism include *The Playwright as Thinker* (1946), *The Dramatic Event* (1954) and *The Life of the Drama* (1967).

NORMAND BERLIN: Professor of English in the University of Massachusetts at Amherst; his publications include *The Secret Cause: A Discussion of Tragedy* (1981) and *Eugene O'Neill* (1982, in the Macmillan Modern Dramatists series).

C. W. E. BIGSBY: Professor of American Studies in the University of East Anglia; his publications include the three-volume study, *A Critical Introduction to Twentieth-Century American Drama* (1982).

TRAVIS BOGARD: Professor of Dramatic Art in the University of California at Berkeley. His *Contour in Time: The Plays of Eugene O'Neill* (1972) has been revised and reissued in paperback (1988); and he has written important Introductions for *The Later Plays of Eugene O'Neill* (1967), *'The Theatre We Worked For': The Letters of Eugene O'Neill to Kenneth Macgowan* (1982), and *'Love and Admiration and Respect': The O'Neill–Commins Correspondence* (1986); he edited *Eugene O'Neill: Complete Plays* (1988).

JOHN MASON BROWN (1900–69): distinguished drama critic of the *New York Evening Post*, the *New York World Telegram* and the *Saturday Review of Literature*, and the author of many books on drama.

ROBERT BRUSTEIN: Artistic Director of the American Repertory Theatre in Boston, Massachusetts, and formerly dean of the Yale Drama School. Drama critic of the *New Republic*, he is the author of many books of theatre criticism, including *The Theatre of Revolt* (1964).

FREDERIC I. CARPENTER: Professor Emeritus of English in the University of California at Berkeley; his publications include *Eugene O'Neill* (1979).

JOHN CHAPMAN (1900–72): influential drama critic for the *New York Daily News*.

JEAN CHOTHIA: Lecturer in English in the University of Cambridge; her publications include *Forging a Language: A Study of the Plays of Eugene O'Neill* (1979).

ST JOHN ERVINE (1883–1971): Irish playwright, novelist, biographer and literary critic, he was drama critic for the *Observer* (1919–23) and other London newspapers between the wars and a critic-commentator for the BBC from 1932.

ROBERT B. HEILMAN: Professor Emeritus of English in the University of Washington at Seattle; his publications include *Tragedy and Melodrama* (1968) and *The Iceman, The Arsonist and The Troubled Agent: Tragedy and Melodrama on the Modern Stage* (1973).

WALTER KERR: influential drama critic for the *New York Herald Tribute* and the *New York Times*; author of many books on drama, including *Tragedy and Comedy* (1968).

JOSEPH WOOD KRUTCH (1893–1970): distinguished drama critic of the *Nation*; his publications on drama include *The American Drama since 1918* (1939) and *The Modern Temper* (1929).

MICHAEL MANHEIM: Professor of English in the University of Toledo, Ohio; his publications include *Eugene O'Neill's New Language of Kinship* (1982).

GEORGE JEAN NATHAN (1882–1958): eminent drama critic for the *Smart Set* magazine and the *American Mercury* (which he edited with H. L. Mencken). His numerous influential reviews have been collected in many volumes.

JOSÉ QUINTERO: the most important director of O'Neill's plays, with landmark productions in 1956 of *The Iceman Cometh* and *Long Day's Journey Into Night*.

JOHN HENRY RALEIGH: Professor of English in the University of California at Berkeley; his publications include *The Plays of Eugene O'Neill* (1965) and the volume of selected criticism on *The Iceman Cometh* in the 'Twentieth-Century Interpretations' series (1968).

TIMO TIUSANEN (1936–85): formerly Professor of Theatre Research in the University of Helsinki, and stage director of plays by O'Neill, Dürrenmatt and Arthur Miller; his publications include *O'Neill's Scenic Images* (1968).

EGIL TORNQVIST: Professor of Scandinavian Studies in the University of Amsterdam; his publications include *A Drama of Souls: Studies in O'Neill's Super-Naturalistic Technique* (1969).

KENNETH TYNAN (1927–80): influential drama critic for the *Spectator*, the *Observer* and the *New Yorker*, and Literary Manager of the National Theatre in London from 1963 to 1973. His dramatic criticism has been collected in several volumes, including *Curtains* (1961), *The Sound of Two Hands Clapping* (1975) and *A View of the English Stage, 1944–63* (1975).

FREDERICK C. WILKINS: Professor of English in Suffolk University, Boston, Mass. Founder and editor of the *Eugene O'Neill Newsletter*, he has written numerous reviews of performances and books relating to O'Neill.

RAYMOND WILLIAMS (1921–88): eminent critic of drama and society, and successively Reader and Professor of Drama in the University of Cambridge from 1961 to 1984. Among his many influential publications are *Drama from Ibsen to Brecht* (1968), *Modern Tragedy* (1966) and *Drama in Performance* (1954).

STARK YOUNG (1881–1963): influential drama critic for the *New Republic* and distinguished essayist, novelist and translator.

ACKNOWLEDGEMENTS

The editor and publishers wish to thank the following for permission to use copyright material: Brooks Atkinson, reviews from issues 27.10.31, 10.10.46 and 9.5.56 and 'Feuding Again', 25.4.48, *The New York Times*, by permission of the New York Times Company. Copyright © 1931, 1946, 1948 and 1956 by the New York Times Company; Judith E. Barlow, extract from *Final Acts* (1985), by permission of the University of Georgia Press. Copyright © 1985 by the University of Georgia Press; Robert Benchley, review in issue 7.11.31, *The New Yorker*, by permission of The New Yorker. Copyright © 1931 by The New Yorker, Inc.; Eric Bentley, extracts from *In Search of Theater* (1955), by permission of Laurence Pollinger Ltd on behalf of the author; C. E. E. Bigsby, extracts from *Twentieth-Century American Drama*, vol. 1, 1900–1940 (1982), by permission of Cambridge University Press; Travis Bogard, extracts from *Contour in Time: The Plays of Eugene O'Neill* (1972), by permission of Oxford University Press, Inc. Copyright © 1972 by Oxford University Press Inc.; John Mason Brown, extract from *Dramatis Personae* (1965), by permission of Viking Penguin Inc. Copyright © 1933 by John Mason Brown; Robert Brustein, extract from *The Theatre of Revolt* (1962), by permission of Little, Brown and Company. Copyright © 1962, 1963, 1964 by Robert Brustein; Jackson R. Bryer, extract from a letter from Eugene O'Neill to Kenneth Macgowan in *The Theatre We Worked For*, Yale University Press, by permission of the Collection of American Literature, The Beinecke Rare Book and Manuscript Library, Yale University; Frederic I. Carpenter, extract from *Eugene O'Neill* (1979), Twayne Publishers, by permission of G. K. Hall & Co.; John Chapman, review from issue 8.11.56, *New York Daily News* (1956), by permission of New York News Inc. Copyright © 1956 by New York News Inc.; J. Chothia, extracts from *Forging a Language* (1979), by permission of Cambridge University Press; Barrett Clark, extract from *European Theories of the Drama* (1943), by permission of Crown Publishers, Inc. Copyright © 1943 by Barrett Clark; St John Ervine, article 'Counsels of Despair', 10.4.48, *Times Literary Supplement*, by permission of Times Newspapers Ltd. Copyright © 1948 by Times Newspapers Ltd; Robert Heilman, extracts from *The Iceman, The Arsonist* and *The Troubled Agent* (1973), by permission of University of Washington Press; Walter Kerr, review in 8.11.56, *New York Herald Tribune*, by permission of the author; Joseph Wood

Krutch, extract from his Introduction to *Nine Plays by Eugene O'Neill* (1932), by permission of Random House, Inc.; Lawrence Langner, extract from *The Magic Curtain* (1951), E. P. Dutton, by permission of Mrs Lawrence Langner. Copyright © 1951 by Lawrence Langner; Michael Manheim, extract from *Eugene O'Neill's New Language of Kinship* (1982), by permission of Syracuse University Press; Seymour Peck, extract from article 'Talking with Mrs. O'Neill', 4.11.56, *The New York Times*, by permission of the New York Times Company. Copyright © 1956 by the New York Times Company; John Henry Raleigh, extract from *The Plays of Eugene O'Neill* (1965), by permission of Southern Illinois University Press; Karl Schriftgriesser, extract from 'Interview with O'Neill', 6.10.46, *The New York Times*, by permission of the New York Times Company. Copyright © 1946 by the New York Times Company; Timo Tiusanen, extracts from *O'Neill Scenic Images* (1968), Princeton University Press, by permission of Ritra Tiusanen; Egil Tornqvist, an extract from *A Drama of Souls* (1969), by permission of Yale University Press; Kenneth Tynan, reviews from issues 2.2.58 and 28.9.58, *The Observer*, by permission of The Observer; Frederick C. Wilkins, extracts from a review in *The Eugene O'Neill Newsletter*, Winter 1985, by permission of the author; Raymond Williams, extract from *Modern Tragedy* (1966), by permission of Chatto & Windus Ltd and Stanford University Press; Stark Young, extract from a review of '*Morning*' in *Immortal Shadows*, (1948), by permission of Charles Scribner's Sons. Copyright © 1948 Charles Scribner's Sons, renewed 1976 by Lewis M. Isaacs, Jr.

Every effort has been made to trace all the copyright holders but if any have been inadvertently overlooked the publishers will be pleased to make the necessary arrangement at the first opportunity.

INDEX

Page numbers in **bold** type denote essays or extracts in this casebook.